CAUSE CÉLÈBRE
A BIOGRAPHY OF
BEVIL JOHN RUDD

LIN MEHMEL AND PATRICK STREETER

John Rudd, the young Guards officer, December 1948

CAUSE CÉLÈBRE
A BIOGRAPHY OF
BEVIL JOHN RUDD

LIN MEHMEL AND PATRICK STREETER

The Matching Press
Harlow
United Kingdom

Published by
The Matching Press
1 Watermans End
Matching Green
Harlow
Essex
CM17 0RQ
UK
Tel 44 (0) 1279 731308
Email Sptstreeter@aol.com
In South Africa, P.O.Box 99 Groot Drakenstein 7680, The Cape
Tel (021) 867 0890
Email Lmehmel@mweb.co.za

Printed by
The Printing Place
14 Hanbury Rd, Chelmsford CM1 3AE, UK

British Library Cataloguing in Publication Data
Cause Célèbre
A Biography of Bevil John Rudd
Softback ISBN 13-978-0-9518664-6-7
Hardback ISBN 13-978-0-9518664-7-4

CONTENTS

Authors' Preface

The authors would like to thank the many people who have helped with this book. In particular, Anna de Lagarda, who was unsparing with her time and put at our disposal all of the large John Rudd archive. Henry Rudd was unstinting with his assistance and encouragement. James Barraclough and Robert Sharp were first-class editors. Others who helped were David Veitch, Achim von Arnem, the late John Kalmanson, the late Lord Balfour of Inchrye, The Earl of Crawford, Nick Ciolli, Tessa Fleischer, Trish Fullerton, Jack Lunger, Alex Knoop, Helen Birks, Penny Hatfield of Eton College Archives, Meirian Jump of the Marx Memorial Library, Mark Paterson and Wendy Edgerley of Woodcote Park School, Rebecca Evans of the London Library, Tatu Laubscher, Monika Duda, Eve Ward Thomas, Andrea Weiss, Charles Rudd, Tom Rudd, Pippa Rudd, John Seekings, Bob Holden, The Hon Gilpatrick Devlin, The Hon Robert Loder, Bongi Maswangani, the late Stanley Uys, Randolph Vigne and Paul Bailey.

This volume must be regarded as work-in-progress. It contains errors and omissions. Also there are many more John Rudd letters, articles and anecdotes out there. Would readers be kind enough to send in anything of interest. If this edition sells well then they can be included in a following one.

Lin Mehmel and Patrick Streeter
Watermans End Cottage
Matching Green
Harlow
Essex, CM17 0RQ, UK
Email Sptstreeter@aol.com
Telephone 44 (0) 1279 731308

List of Illustrations

Rudd Family Tree

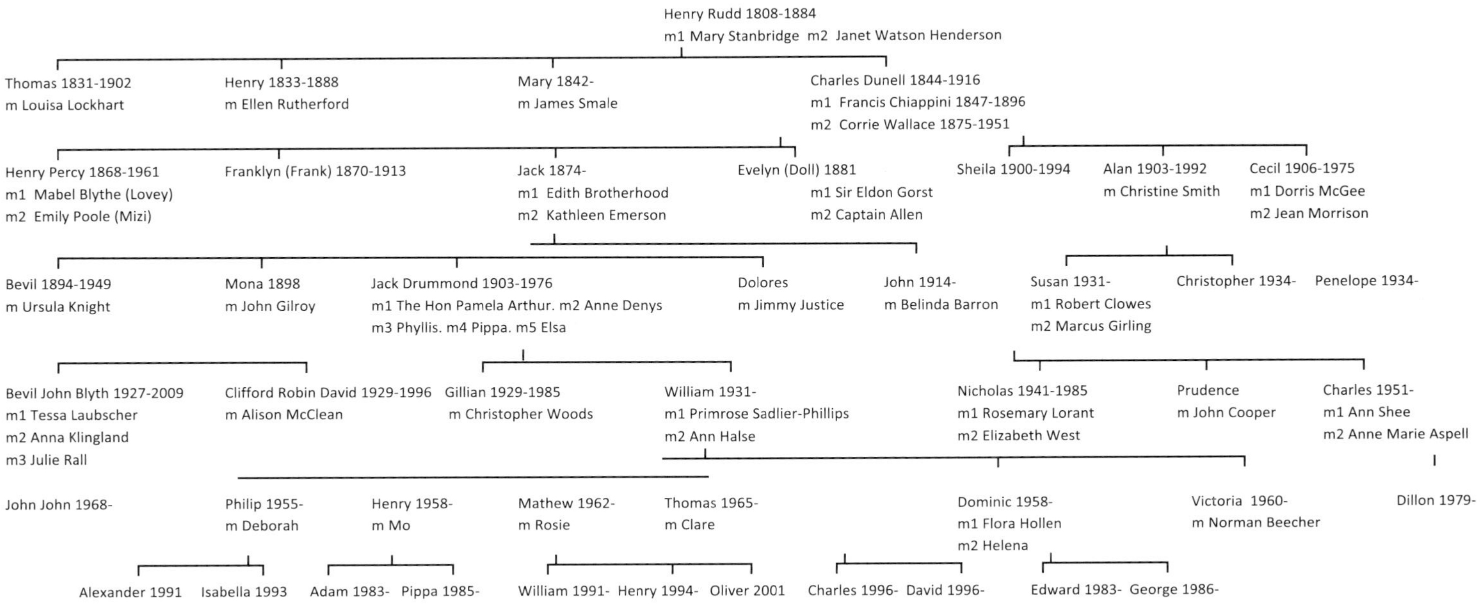

CHAPTER ONE

ORIGINS

A smart lunch party was assembling at one of those incomparable Dutch farm houses in the Franschhoek valley of the Cape, South Africa early in 2001. There was a rustle of excitement within the assembled guests as one of their number, who had yet to arrive, had a whiff of notoriety about him. He was John Rudd, an Old Etonian member of South Africa's mining aristocracy. Suddenly he appeared, not through the door but through a French window. He was a good-looking man for his early seventies, now balding, but with a shock of hair that stuck up like Struwwelpeter's. Immediately he electrified the assembly with his quick-fire conversation, noticeable for its ability to dart from one topic to another. What was his mystery? Well, 40 years earlier he had been involved in a romance across South Africa's racial divide, at that time a 'crime'. John and his then true love had been tried, convicted and imprisoned for six months.

But where did the Rudds come from? How did they rise to the pantheon of the Randlords, that collective word for the elite of the diamond mines and gold fields? The patriarch was Charles, born in Norfolk in 1844. The family were shipbuilders from Sunderland, but Charles's father was the younger son of a younger son and enjoyed little inheritance. Instead he made his own way, trading with South Africa as a merchant. He was prosperous enough to give his son a good education, first at a preparatory school in Wadhurst, Surrey and then at Harrow, where he flourished as an athlete and was the champion Racquets player. He won the school mile and the competition for throwing the cricket ball, but an accident to his hand prevented him playing at Lord's against Eton. He went on to Trinity College, Cambridge, winning both the singles and doubles Racquets championships; however, training for athletics, he over-extended himself and damaged his health. Abandoning his studies, he travelled to South Africa to regain his strength. First he went on safari with John Dunn, a white hunter and Zulu chief, and later joined a hunting expedition with a German adventurer Eduard Mohr, but he was struck down with malaria and travelled to Ceylon to recover. Back in Africa in 1868, he set up as a merchant in Durban, and a year later, three years after diamonds were first found, we find him working the riverbeds on the diamond fields. At first, times were hard for Charles; he lived in a ragged tent and survived on the most basic food, then he was struck down with typhoid and had to return to Cape Town to recover. He later moved on to the dry diggings, but suffered another setback when a parcel of diamonds for which he was responsible was stolen. Later, in 1871, he met Cecil Rhodes, when they shared a quarter claim in Baxter's Gully. There was a nine year age gap but Rhodes was always mature for his age, so this did not matter. Indeed, the two men had a lot in common - a solid middle-class background, a thirst for adventure, a sense of humour and a love of the Classics. Charles cut an imposing figure. He was described as 'a tall erect man, slender in build, having dark eyes, thick fair hair, and a well-trimmed dark beard'. They worked their claims together, as well as operating pumping and ice-making machinery. Charles wrote later about the ice-making machine, 'I am fairly certain Rhodes arrived at the fields in May 1871. He and I ordered an ice-making machine together in 1871, it was disappointingly long in arriving, but it ultimately landed at Cape Town and we got it up by mule wagon at a cost of 55 shillings per 100lbs. It arrived in January 1872. February and March were record wet months and an early winter set in, we were nearly ruined. The following summer was especially hot, and the machine paid for itself in three months, and we sold it at the end of the summer for more than it cost. Rhodes had some money but this £1,500 for ice was my first capital, and I put it into Baxter's Gully – De Beers'. From then on Charles's business prospered and he managed both their business affairs while Rhodes was at Oxford. In 1880, together with Rhodes, he founded the De Beers Mining Company, which gradually consolidated the mines. Also he represented Kimberley in the Cape parliament and by 1886 was a rich man.

In 1886, Charles accompanied Rhodes to view the newly discovered gold fields. After a hesitant start, when Charles felt the fields had been 'salted', the two of them founded, and became joint Managing Directors of, The Gold Fields of South Africa Ltd. Two years later, Charles led the expedition to King Lobengula of the Matabele to negotiate the Rudd Concession for mineral rights. He was accompanied by Francis 'Matabele' Thompson and James Rochfort Maguire. Also in the party were Charles's 18 year-old son Frank, a friend of Frank's, called Denny, and six servants. Thompson had been born

Charles Rudd aged 24 and his wife, Fanny Chiappini in 1868, shortly before he left for the diamond fields

on the high seas off Port Elizabeth 31 years earlier. As a boy he had witnessed, in a raid by Chief Galeshiwe of the Ngqikas, the murder of his father and the burning of their farm. He was also seriously wounded and these traumas made him, under stress, sometimes lose his nerve. However, he was accomplished in the skills of the outback and spoke some of the native languages. His eldest son, Neville Rudd Thompson was killed on the north-western frontier in India in 1915. Later he became a moderate member of the Cape Parliament and eventually retired to his farm, Cornforth Hill in the Northern Cape, where he died in 1927. Maguire was a strange choice as he was an unworldly academic. A qualified lawyer with a double first from Oxford in maths and law, apparently he was so impractical that he could not open a tin of salmon. However, the skills of the three were complementary and no doubt Rhodes thought Maguire would draft any agreement in good legal language and that some of his classical culture would rub off on Thompson. Maguire later became an Irish Nationalist MP and was President of the British South Africa Company from 1923 until 1925 when he died.

When they arrived at the King's kraal in Bulawayo, they found three other parties also seeking a concession. Eventually, Rhodes was to buy all three out. The negotiations with the King were longwinded and then Sir Sidney Shippard, the UK Government's representative in Bechuanaland, arrived on the scene. He was there to investigate a recent murder. Lobengula wanted to consult Sir Sidney and so kept Charles and his party waiting. Fortunately, Sir Sidney was a friend of Rhodes, so with his help and with the enticing inducement of 1,000 Martini-Henry rifles, 100,000 rounds and a gun-boat to defend the Zambesi, the concession was, after 29 days of negotiation, agreed and signed. The gun-boat was never delivered.

Thompson stayed on in Bulawayo for a year so as to ensure the terms were carried out. On his way back with the document, Charles decided to take a short cut but got lost in the bush where his horse fell on him. Almost dying of thirst, he was rescued by two wandering natives. Wilbur Smith, in his novel *Men of Men,* includes Charles as a character when recounting the opening up of the mines and the capture of Rhodesia. The Rudd concession led to the founding of the British South African Company whose territory later became Rhodesia.

During the 1890s, Charles spent much of his time in London managing the affairs of the Gold Fields Company, which had now become *The Consolidated Gold Fields of South Africa Ltd.* He managed to keep the company clear of scandals following the Jameson Raid, the ill-fated attempted *coup d'état* by Rhodes and Dr Jameson on the Transvaal republic. He wrote that the news that Consolidated Goldfields was part of the raid came upon him like a thunderclap. He feared that Kruger would confiscate all the Company's property and concluded that it could only have been organized by a madman. Many people think that the raid ended the friendship between Rhodes and Charles but in fact it continued and Rhodes would often stay with Charles at his Scottish estate. Both he and Dr Jameson came to the house-warming, or rather castle-warming, party at Glenborrodale Castle in August 1901. Guests were distressed to see Rhodes gasping for breath and he was to die the following year.

In his mid-fifties, Charles reduced his business commitments and concentrated on his estate at Ardnamurchan, Argyllshire, where he built Glenborrodale Castle.

He was also a sponsor of science and an expert on ferns, of which he had a fine collection. He funded a study of the mammals of South Africa with specimens going to the Natural History Museum in South Kensington. A tropical bird, *Rudd Apalis,* and a flower, *Penstemon Charles Rudd,* were named after him. He was a quiet, taciturn man who did not court publicity. Sometime after Rhodes's death he threw a chest of his papers into the sea saying, "There go the secrets of the Jameson Raid." He gave away much of

Glenborrodale Castle, Ardnamurchan

his fortune anonymously to the Mount Vernon Hospital and other charities. £200,000, which in today's money is about £17M, went to the hospital. His first wife, Frances, died in 1896, and two years later, aged 54, he proposed to Corrie Wallace, a daughter of an old friend of his from Kimberley days who was thirty years younger than him. In fact, his son Percy had earlier proposed to her and been refused. His first proposal was also refused but a later one was successful and they started a second family. Of this family his daughter Sheila was the most interesting. She was named after the place where they were living, Shiel Bridge. She was born in 1900 and so was six years younger than her nephew, Bevil. She grew up in Scotland where her father had great wealth and they spent the winters in Bournemouth. As a child she saw the *Titanic* sail out of Southampton. She reacted against the family money and in her late teens joined the Communist Party. She visited the Soviet Union for six months in 1925 with a group of intellectuals. There is a family story that she had a Russian lover and that their letters were stopped by the authorities. She lived modestly and never gave up her socialist beliefs. When the Berlin Wall fell she remarked, 'Just wait, capitalism will not be far behind'. She was a talented sculptress and drove ambulances in London during the Blitz. After

Charles Rudd with his second family: Sheila, who became a Communist, and later an accomplished sculptress and archaeologist, Alan, Corrie and Cecil

her mother died in 1951 she emigrated to Rhodesia and took up archaeology. She excavated Mount Tsindi, 60 kilometres east of Harare. Well into her seventies she would boast that she could out dig all the University students who came to help her. Her rows with her fellow archaeologists were legend and her life's work was published in 1984. She died in 1994 leaving a few thousand pounds to her four great-great nephews. The family assumed that the bulk of her estate went to President Mugabe or some similar nationalist cause.

Charles died, following a fall on his estate, in 1916, aged 72. Corrie later married a nephew of Rhodes's, but he was a wastrel, or as Rhodes would have said, "a loafer", and she had difficulty extricating herself from the entanglement.

Charles had seven children and the eldest was John's grandfather Percy. Percy had the reputation of being difficult, gloomy and cantankerous. At the age of 26 he was taken seriously ill and given six months to live. In fact he lived to 92, but was invariably lugubrious and expecting to die. His son Bevil waited for him to die as he thought he would inherit his seat on the De Beers board, but in fact Percy outlived him by twelve years. Percy followed his father to Harrow and then went up to Oxford. He aimed for a diplomatic career but, while on holiday in South Africa, enlisted in the Cape Town Highlanders, then transferred to the Royal Scots Guards and served in Malta and England. He left the Army in 1897 to train with De Beers and, on Rhodes's suggestion, became his alternate director, serving on the board until his death 61 years

Charles Rudd in later life

later. For the son of a Randlord he lived modestly in the Rudd bungalow in Kimberley, his only extravagances being racehorses and shooting. The bungalow is still there and, according to the Kimberley tourist guide, it is now haunted. A lady in white appears on the balcony, there are at least six ghosts of servants in the courtyard and Percy himself haunts the sick room.

Percy had two sons and two daughters and the elder son, Bevil, was John's father. In every department Bevil was an exemplary man: a charismatic father,

Three generations of the Rudd family outside the Rudd Bungalow in Kimberley, Charles with his son Percy and, to the left, Percy's wife Mabel. Young Bevil stands between his father and a lady who is probably his aunt. It is interesting to note how the dog resembles his owner.

world sporting hero and brave officer in the First World War. He was born in 1894 and educated at St. Andrew's College, Grahamstown, from where he won a Rhodes scholarship to Trinity College, Oxford. Immediately on the outbreak of war in 1914 he joined the Argyll and Sutherland Highlanders as a Second Lieutenant. One of his letters to his parents from the Western Front survives. He wrote, *'I have spent the longest day I have ever known today – the Germans began to make things lively with aerial torpedoes and trench mortars filled with shrapnel. I had just had lunch and felt the wretched monotony of things when an appalling crash woke me up. It was an aerial torpedo about 200 yards away. You cannot imagine what uncanny things they are – they make no noise and you can watch them coming, shaped like a*

Champagne bottle, in a slow half-circle containing immense quantities of dynamite. They steer themselves, thin end first and then dive, bursting when they reach the ground. The roar is deafening.'

Later, he transferred to the Tank Corps where he won the MC at the battle of Cambrai. The citation said, 'As an officer commanding six tanks he saved a difficult situation by courage and skill'. Miraculously, he survived the war unscathed, except when he was concussed in an accident, but, like so many combatants, he was mentally troubled by his experiences. Many years later on Remembrance Day, his widow Ursula wrote down how much that day meant to Bevil. He would never miss visiting the Cenotaph. She recalled what a terrible thing the First World War was to him. Philip Noel-Baker, a fellow athlete and John's godfather, recalled that Bevil was a special kind of war casualty. Physically he got through but was fundamentally shocked by it. Bevil, he said, had a quality of innocence and later never recovered from the traumas. After the war, he returned to Oxford where he excelled as an athlete and was approached by both the UK and South African authorities to represent them at the 1920 Olympic Games in Antwerp. He chose South Africa and won the gold in the 400 meters, silver in the 400 meters relay and a bronze in the 800 meters, the only South African to win a full set. These triumphs made him a national hero, a mantle he wore with considerable modesty.

In 1921, he took up a position teaching English and History at Harrow School. Terence Rattigan, a pupil, remembered his good looks and panache, particularly as he would attend lessons still dressed in white tie and tails from the previous night out in London. Recently his twin great-grandsons were at the school. There were plans to present his medals there but in the end they have gone to Bevil's old school, St. Andrew's College, Grahamstown. His next position was as Private Secretary to the Earl of Birkenhead, a friend of Churchill and Lord Chancellor. He first met Birkenhead at the University Sports Day. He touched the quarter-mile tape in a memorable dead-heat with Guy Butler and collapsed fainting into Birkenhead's arms. This incident persuaded him that Bevil would make a good Private Secretary. He accompanied Birkenhead, or F.E. as he was often called, on a trip to America where Bevil was already a popular hero following his win there in an international half-mile race when his burst at the straight electrified the 100,000 crowd. As F.E.'s son records in his biography of his father, Bevil was

Bevil winning the 400 metres Gold Medal at the 1920 Antwerp Olympic Games

a charming, gentle, but eccentric character, more at home on the track than with the typewriter. He was distracted at the time by a series of unrequited love affairs and seldom went to bed, but would lurk in the sitting room until dawn. Then he would fall asleep at inconvenient moments during the working day with his mouth wide open. F.E.'s daughter Lady Eleanor Smith and her friend Zita Jungman, who were on the tour, would pop lumps of sugar in it and joyfully watch them melt. F.E. tolerated this charming but unconventional assistant of whom he was fond and whose talents he admired. But his patience was stretched when, at 7.30 am on a railway journey, a large black Pullman waiter approached carrying a tray with a double whisky-and–soda and two aspirins.

"What is that?" he asked.

"Massa Rudd's breakfast, Sah," came the reply. F.E. was annoyed by this incident which would do nothing to repair Bevil's inefficiency, but the latter made amends by producing a letter from a young lady fan of F.E.'s in which she extolled her attractions. When the Birkenhead family were holidaying in

Scotland, Bevil would accompany them when out riding by running alongside the horses and spurting ahead to open the gates.

Bevil was next employed as a sports journalist for the *Argus* newspapers in South Africa and then worked for De Beers, but his unworldliness meant he was never suitable for, or interested in, a high position. John describes an incident when he was a diamond sorter and was working late in the sorting office and fell asleep in the washroom and was locked in. He felt this was a misdemeanour and greatly surprised Sir Ernest Oppenheimer, his boss, by suggesting in a gentlemanly way that his bonus be reduced.

Bevil's relations with his father were strained. Jack, the other son, an improvident playboy who was married five times, was the favourite. Percy kept Bevil's family short of money and there may have been problems with his drinking. Extraordinarily, it would appear that the elder man was jealous of his son and also he took against his charming and inoffensive wife, Ursula. During the Second World War, Bevil served with the Intelligence Corps in London and after the war he returned to Kimberley to work in a modest position for De Beers. He died in 1948, at the early age of 53, following an operation for a duodenal ulcer. After Bevil's death Percy's meanness of spirit came to the fore when he asked the newly widowed Ursula to repay the money that Bevil owed him. Ivor Thomas, a Labour MP and also an international runner, wrote to *The Times* thus,

'Bevil Rudd, whose unexpected early death in South Africa was announced in The Times recently, was perhaps the greatest natural athlete of our day. If he had not entirely devoted himself to the track, his early promise at Cricket and Rugby Football would surely have won him equal fame at these sports. His all-round performance in the University Sports of 1920 – when beaten in the 100 yards by less than a foot in every time by Harold Abrahams, won the half-mile from E.D.Mountain in 1 min. 57 2-5 seconds, dead-heated with Guy Butler in the quarter-mile in 49 3-5 seconds and withal found time to get a place in the long jump. All in the same afternoon – eclipses even his Olympic victory in the 400 meters in the same year. In action on his day he was superb. But he will be remembered also by many as one of the most clubbable men of his generation, whether in many of his formal clubs or in the many groups of his private friends. The Trinity Claret Club and the Vincent's (of which he was President), at Oxford, the United Services Club and the Athenaeum, in London,

were only a few of the many places where his genial personality radiated good humour. He was fortunate in his marriage to Miss Ursula Knight, and happy in seeing his two sons showing his own prowess: for both of them played in the Eton XI, one being Captain. It is strange that the boon companion of his running days, E.A.Montague, should have died about the same time. Athletes of this generation will always think of themselves together. 'They were lovely and pleasant in their lives, and in death they are not divided; they were swifter than eagles, they were stronger than lions'.

John was born on the 7th April 1927 in the Rudd Bungalow in Kimberley. This is in Edgerton Road in the suburb of Belgravia. When Charles Rudd acquired it in 1896, it had just four rooms. During the Boer War it was hit by a shell. It was passed to Percy in 1898 and grew to accommodate the family needs. It was in the dining room with old satin walls and huge Victorian cupboards that he used to regale his grandchildren with stories of Rhodes's visits and the happenings of the old mining days. When Percy died in 1961, it passed to his widow and then to her sister, who sold the furniture, and later, in 1968, the house. De Beers were persuaded by Dr Richard Liversidge of the McGregor Museum to purchase it. It was then, under John's guidance, restored and opened to the public in 1988. At the time of John's birth, his parents were living with his grandparents. John's mother, Ursula, was the daughter of Clifford Knight, a successful Cape merchant, and his wife Edith. John described Ursula as the sheet-anchor of the family. She was capable, homely and protective, not the dazzling kind of person Bevil might have married to his cost. She would make clothes and wanted the very best for her boys who were the focus of her life. Her greatest fear was that drink might corrupt those dear to her.

John's first school was Woodcote House, Windlesham, Surrey which he would have entered about 1935, when the family were living in England, and Bevil had taken a job as athletics correspondent for *The Daily Telegraph*. At first they lived in Chalfont St. Peter and later moved to the Old Town in Beaconsfield. Across the road lived G.K.Chesterton; his enormous size used to delight them all as he got on and off the bus that plied between the Old and New Town. Judging from his letters home and the school reports, John was happy at the new school. The setting of the school buildings in fine grounds on the edge of the Surrey village of Windlesham is very English. Although

Woodcote House School
First X1 Team 1939

R B Bennett R Dearden K Adlard D Antill
B J B Rudd M W O Anthill D Lewis (Capt) N M Moorhead B Bagnal
I Phillpotts C R D Rudd

The 1939 First Eleven Cricket Team at John's first school, Woodcote House. John's brother Robin, a precocious cricketer, was also in the team. He went on to captain Eton and play for Oxford.

in a brief memoir he mentions the usual horrors, knuckles hit with toothbrushes and beatings at the hands of school bullies, his letters list skating, riding, racing and athletics as his interests. The school is still going and has been owned by the Paterson family since 1931. Mark Paterson, then a pupil and later a headmaster, now in his 92nd year, remembers the Rudd brothers and their prowess at cricket Particularly interesting is a short analysis of the international situation written by John at the time of Munich. He decides that clearly appeasement has no future and that war, although horrific, is necessary. In 1939 the family returned to South Africa. Bevil thought the job prospects might be better there; his father was over 70 and there was talk of him replacing him on the De Beers board. They drove up from the Cape to Kimberley, then a journey of three to four days involving frequent stops to unlock farm gates. They spent some time at the De Beers shooting lodge in the veld and then back to the Cape, where he attended for a few terms Western Province Prep School in Claremont. John recalled at the outbreak of war, hearing the news of the sinking of the *Athenia* from the radios in the shops in Adderley Street, and the German Ambassador telling Percy in the Mount Nelson Hotel that he could have his table temporarily but that he would want it back.

CHAPTER TWO

ETON AND SANDHURST

In 1940, John sailed back to England alone, the ship zig-zagging across the seas, so as to avoid mines and submarines, and he entered Oliver Van Oss's house at Eton. Eton was Ursula's idea as she had high expectations for her boys. It broke with tradition as previously six Rudds had gone to Harrow, but now, starting with John's brother Robin, seven more were to follow there, three of them playing in the Cricket XI. But Harrow regained its place in 2009 when Robin's twin grandsons, Charles and David, started there. They were intended for Eton, who lost their entry papers, and they were to thrive at Harrow.

John's reports at school took a turn for the worse, a usual occurrence for thirteen-year-olds. World-weary schoolmasters have a delightful style when writing about the delinquents in their charge. Oliver Van Oss wrote,

'Next half he will find all sorts of nasty land-mines going off under him if doesn't do much better. I foresee a major explosion after about a month, followed by great improvement. Apart from this I think he is a grand boy; lively and straightforward, with plenty of devil in him. There is no doubt that his cricket is promising.'

John's first Form Master was Peter Blundell and he also wrote woefully of John. In 1942, while serving as Captain in the Kings Royal Rifle Corps he was killed in action. John wrote in his diary of him,

'The list of fallen officers in The Times includes Captain P.C. Blundell, K.R.R.C. Feeling very sorry indeed, most tragic, because of all I remember about him in the summer of 1940, in his house, garden, restoring order in the pupil room, signing thirteen rips, Corps mornings, I know there could be no greater loss. I remember our last handshake in his room. He jumped down the stairs in slippers and got a bit red and hoarse, and at once asked me where I was going and all sorts of homely questions about the holidays and how he thought I would do better next half. I shall see that when I am in the 16 inch turret of a battleship, or cockpit of a Hurricane, or bomb-aimer of a Stirling. I won't forget to mutter, "That's for Peter Blundell K.R.R.C". We don't discuss it, but we all know how he felt.'

John was delighted to find a local link with South Africa when he discovered that one of the Thames Watermen had fought in the Boer War. He had been at Jagersfontein and Kimberley. He also taught himself to forge his Housemaster's signature - a useful ability, but there is no evidence that he put this skill to use. An excitement occurred at Eton when it was noticed that sums of money were going missing. Marked coins were left as a trap and a boy called Wilkie was caught and obliged to leave.

The Rudd Family during World War Two, Bevil, Ursula, Robin and John

As John worked his way up the school, his reports hardly improved. In 1944, he played in the Eton and Harrow cricket match. As it was wartime, the match was played on the Harrow ground and not at Lord's. Eton were a strong side and reached the Harrow total of 147 with a loss of 5 wickets. Robin was also in the team and scored 29 not out, but John did not bat. Robin was to go on to captain the Eton team and play for Oxford. John gained one wicket when he trapped the Harrow captain Jackson lbw for 7 runs. Van Oss wrote, 'I think very highly of him, not least for the way he can take punishment.' The English master, Routh, wrote,

'It is almost impossible for me to write a report about this boy because he has seldom been in school, hardly at all in the last three weeks. When he has

been there I have the uneasy feeling that he has been more concerned in maintaining his reputation as a "funny fellow" than he has been concerned with English and European history. Sometimes he is amusing and even witty, but he comes perilously near to becoming a buffoon.'

His Science report was no better,

'He is not much interested in Science or its applications. His written answers are but little more than a regurgitation of undigested matter.'

Van Oss summed it all up by saying, 'He'll always be up to some mischief or other, thank goodness, but there is not an atom of vice in him. I like him a lot'. Another aspect of John is recorded in the House Book, which was written up by the boys. He starts off well, being described as quiet and sensible and promising at cricket, but by the next term he is accused of 'needless insubordination'. The following year he redeems himself on the football field, where he is noted as an excellent keeper who has welded a rabble into an experienced side. In his last year, John is responsible for writing up the records. He records how Rudd Major misjudged a long hop and played it back into Hill-Wood's hands. A team mate felt this was incomplete and added, 'As Rudd has done the same thing almost every innings this year the word "misjudged" is inappropriate. He took a colossal swoosh showing a lack of situation that was criminal'. But John's Eton games career ended in triumph. As well as cricket, he played in the school first rugger and football teams and was javelin champion, winning his athletics colours. His Eton career was topped off when Ian Gilmour proposed him for Pop, the exclusive club of the social and sporting elite.

Ursula with John and Robin, two Eton cricketers

John had happy memories

SWORD OF HONOUR

B.J.B. RUDD

October 1945

The Medal and Pin that went with John's Sword of Honour. In later life, in a quixotic gesture, he gave the Sword to a girlfriend and its current whereabouts is unknown

of Eton; he enjoyed the wartime fire-watching and made many friends who lasted throughout his life. He resolved on an Army career and the next port of call was Sandhurst, which was not based at Sandhurst during the war but at Aldershot, where he excelled, winning the Sword of Honour.

John's fellow Cadets were an aristocratic bunch including Colin Tennant, later Lord Glenconner, Robin Balniel, later the Earl of Crawford, and Sir Mark Norman. But much of the life of a Cadet was humdrum: military exercises interrupted by meals of spam. Whenever they travelled, the great game was to avoid buying a ticket and jump over the station barriers. While at Sandhurst he was in the local cinema when a newsflash came over: WAR IS OVER. VE DAY TOMORROW. Suddenly, the Gestapo characters in the film became unimportant. That night the pipes struck up in the barrack square and it filled with men milling in the twilight. The floodlights from army trucks lit everything up and rockets went off. There was a spirit of anarchy. John and Colin Tennant jointly mounted a bicycle and rode it into the crowd. Later, John wandered around in his pyjamas.

The next morning, they were issued with passes and John hitched a lift on the running board of an ambulance; all the Cadets surged down to Brookwood station, where the waiting passengers were six deep on the platform. Not all could get into the train and some travelled, Indian-style, hanging on to the outside. Once in London, John gravitated to Trafalgar Square which was full of people, flags and empty glasses. At 3 o'clock, they heard Churchill's 'Cease Fire' and John fought his way down Whitehall, hoping to see Churchill come out on a balcony. He suddenly appeared, some 30 yards away, driven in a small car. John, by then surrounded by jubilant Poles and Belgians wearing their countries' berets, jumped on the running board of a following police car. It was a hot day, the temperature reaching 84 degrees, and he was roasting in his battle dress, so he decided to retreat to the *Lansdowne Club* in Berkeley Square for a swim. At this point, he met up with some friends, Tim Mosley, Robin Balniel and Bill Young, and they took a taxi to the *Gargoyle Club* at 69 Dean Street, Soho. This was a fashionable, *avant-garde* establishment run by Colin Tennant's uncle David, where the interiors were by Matisse. Here, on the balcony, they feasted off chicken and Champagne and misbehaved by throwing orange peel onto the revellers below. David Tennant had a row with Robert Newton, the actor. Newton was at the height of his fame and was known for playing rough diamonds like Long John Silver and no doubt lived up to his stage persona. John watched David making eyes at the girl in charge of making up the bills. Then David danced with her but this all came to an end when his wife Virginia Parsons arrived. The revellers then made a Victory march past the Ritz, where they found Mark Norman drunk, and on to the Dorchester. John spent the night in the *Lansdowne,* which cost him 12/6d. Robin Balniel and Colin Tennant were turned away on the grounds that the club was full, and spent the night in Hyde Park.

John, Winston Churchill and others celebrating VE Day as portrayed in The Daily Mirror. John is meant to be standing behind Churchill's car but it is difficult to pick him out.

The next day was a time for hangovers and the following one he went home. On the way, he bought a copy of *The Daily Mirror* and was delighted to find a picture of him standing behind Churchill's car.

He was commissioned in the Coldstream Guards, serving in the Fourth Battalion, stationed at Windsor Barracks - a handy posting as he could enjoy London social life. He went to parties with the young Princesses Elizabeth and Margaret and escorted Miss Jacqueline Bouvier when she was in London, maintaining a correspondence when she returned to America. She was very interested in Cecil Rhodes and John sent her the original of one of his letters. She was delighted with it but dared not keep it and sent it back. Her letter back is reproduced in the appendix. One of his tasks was to resolve disputes which broke out in the lower ranks. There was the case of Mrs Kerry, wife of an Irish Guardsman, who had water thrown over her from an upstairs window by Mrs Ayling, wife of a Grenadier, and also the matter of Private Evans whose wife was assaulted with a belt and buckle by a Mr Bagge. Resolving these disputes may have been a good preparation for his next posting, for the Battalion was sent to Palestine where the Jews and the Arabs were at each other's throats and the hapless British were attempting to hold the ring. Ursula sent out copies of *Tatler* to him to keep him up to date with social life back home. He was a conscientious soldier and was wounded in an Irgun explosion and travelled to South Africa to recover. He was left with a slight limp for the rest of his life. He also grasped the political dimension of the problem and had a well-received article published in the *Twentieth Century* magazine.

The ten-page article describes how the security forces had difficulty in counteracting the Jewish terrorism because they, the Irgun Zvai Leumi and the Stern Gang, intimidated the Jewish population and prevented cooperation. Then John goes on to describe a visit to the kibbutz *Ein Harod*. There he found a harsh way of life where all property was held in common, children were separated from their parents from the age of six, and a military ethos pervaded. He found all this distasteful and noted that, in spite of their poverty, he preferred the romantic chaos of the Arab villages. He also described the attack in February 1947 of the Irgun, aided by the Stern Gang, on Citrus House, the British military headquarters in Tel Aviv. The terrorists brought their guns to the houses surrounding Citrus House the day before the raid. After the first volley the soldiers inside grabbed their weapons and manned the windows, blazing away at the enemy in the houses opposite. Some auxiliary Arab policemen accidentally sent some friendly fire into the backs of the British. In a car park opposite was a lorry full of gas canisters which, one by one, exploded, showering down shrapnel. Then the firing subsided; the terrorists had had enough and melted away. It was noted that the Jewish telephonists in the house had been tipped off and left early. The Irgun were not to be defeated. The basement of a barber's shop opposite was rented by a man 'who wanted to store potatoes' and they started to tunnel towards Citrus House. A large quantity of explosives was brought in in potato sacks. There were only a few yards to go and the tunnel was under an area where the troops queued every evening for the NAAFI. Luckily the Haganah, the Jewish Defence Force, and the forerunner of the Israeli Army, discovered the secret and raided the basement and cemented up the tunnel. The Haganah sapper who led the raid was blown up by a booby trap meant for the British. Sixty thousand Jews lined the streets for his funeral. In the article John mentions a 'raven-haired Rachel' who worked in the complex and who took part in the defence of Citrus House. In a letter home he confesses that he was infatuated with her, saying, 'She is the most beautiful female I have ever laid eyes on' and he admits that he is always making excuses to visit her workplace. There is no evidence that his passions were reciprocated.

John went on to describe how he witnessed Jewish terrorism from the front line, and in particular how he saw a badly injured policeman pulled from a bombed building, and noted that the Jewish population refused to help the security services arrest Stern Gang and Irgun members.

Dolores Gray

When his tour of duty in Palestine ended, John was posted to Windsor. There he started to court another celebrity girlfriend - Dolores Gray, a 25 year old American. She was a star of films and stage and was then performing in *Annie Get Your Gun* in the West End; they met at the Royal Empire Society Ball. Dolores is largely forgotten now but at the time was as celebrated as Ethel Merman. One critic described her voice as 'a freight-train slathed in honey'. John took her to the *Trooping of the Colour* and the *Royal Tournament.*

His duties at this time included commanding the guard outside the castle and choosing the band's music. Members of the Royal Family would look down on the proceedings from a window. The Queen conveniently liked music from *Annie Get Your Gun,* but the King preferred *Brigadoon*. In a letter to his grandfather John gives a vivid description of a day when he commanded the Changing of the Guard. He had a close escape when a pigeon just missed his bearskin with a deposit. Then the troop had to negotiate the Windsor traffic as they marched from the barracks to the castle, but buses pulled into the side and policemen saluted as they passed by. The King stood in the Sovereign's Entrance and the Queen and the two Princesses in a large alcove window above. John feared that he would muff his commands but all went well. The band played 'You can't get a man with a gun' from *Annie*. Then there was a lunch with the Royal Family and their guests before they went to the Ascot races. John abandoned his bearskin but was otherwise in full dress. He was ushered along a long gallery manned by footmen to a vast green and gold drawing room, which was full of equerries, some of whom he fortunately knew, and, when the Royal Family came in he was introduced by Piers Legh, one of the equerries. He chatted to Princess Elizabeth, then aged 23 and one year older than himself and he was impressed by her vivacity. When talking to Princess Margaret he noticed her remarkable eyes. At lunch they ate off gold plate and John sat opposite Princess Margaret and between Lady Jean Rankin, a Lady in Waiting, and the Duchess of Beaufort. The Duchess said she knew nothing about racing as she was only there for the food and Lady Jean played 'footy footy' with him under the table. After lunch all the guests departed in carriages for the Ascot races but John had to return to his barracks.

Subsequently, a more mundane task was helping with the breaking of the 1949 Dock Strike. The Coldstreams went down to the docks to unload frozen meat. John was contemplating leaving the Army but his mind was made up for him when, following his earlier wound, he developed osteomyelitis in his leg and he had to resign his commission.

CHAPTER THREE

DIAMONDS AND DRAMA

Now arrived the difficult task of choosing a new career. The obvious choice was De Beers, the family firm co-founded by his great grandfather, where his grandfather was still on the board. Interviews were held in London and Harry Oppenheimer happily agreed to take him on, remarking that he had no business training and would have to start at the bottom. In 1950 he reported to the offices in Main Street, Johannesburg and commenced in the Records Department, later moving to the diamond sorting office. In 1951 he started working as Secretary to Sir Ernest Oppenheimer, the Chairman, then aged 71. Later his brother Robin was to be Harry Oppenheimer's personal assistant.

John at about the time of the Foreshore Case. Note the apartheid notice in the background

Sir Ernest was a business genius. The Oppenheimers were late on the scene for the exploitation of South Africa's diamonds and gold but by the end of the First World War they controlled the industry. Sir Ernest was a benign, avuncular figure and John worshipped him and treated him as a second father. In 1956 John took a further step up the ladder when he was appointed director of the De Beers subsidiary covering South West Africa, now Namibia. He was given charge of a particularly tricky and crucial law case, known as the Foreshore Case, where the South West African government sought to remove the company's rights to offshore mining. He steered the issue to victory.

John was interested in politics but never joined a political party; however, he did join the *Torch Commandos* - a movement set up by returning servicemen to protest against the removal of the vote from the coloured population. He was deeply disturbed by the Sharpeville shootings and, in spite of the swarms of police, drove there the day after to see for himself what had happened. Later he got to know Oliver and Adelaide Tambo when they were in exile in London. One of the Tambos' daughters, Tisane, became John's god-daughter and she recalls how helpful John was while they were refugees and how he always cheered them up. When the ANC and Chief Buthelezi's Inkatha movement parted company he acted as a go-between for the two organisations.

John and Tessa 1955

In 1953, at the age of 26, John married the 19-year-old Tessa Laubscher, a young actress, at St. George's Church, Parkton, Johannesburg. John's friends and family were not entirely happy with the match. Robin, John's brother, argued strongly against it and many of his business colleagues never really accepted her. Her family were Afrikaans. Her father had been born in the veld under a bush during the Boer war, when her grandmother was hiding from the British who were herding women and children into concentration camps. Her mother's father came from Germany and married into the old established de Villiers family. Tessa's father was a doctor working in the Railways Department but he was an Afrikaans speaker and so was discharged from his post and his career suffered greatly. Ironically, when the Nationalists came to power the individual who did this was similarly discharged. World War Two had only ended eight years earlier; anti-German feeling was strong, and there were rumours, totally unfounded, that her family had been Nazi supporters. She was very attractive and had featured as a Rag Queen in a pageant in her home town. John saw her and asked a mutual friend, Ian Calder, to introduce them. They had an extended honeymoon in Europe and for a year they were based in London in a charming flat between Mount Street and Oxford Street. Tessa was a hopeless cook, never having been taught at home, but she made up for this by making all her own clothes and tastefully decorating the flat.

On their return to South Africa, with the help of a £3,000 loan from Harry Oppenheimer, they built *Mingary,* a house in Bryanston, a suburb of Johannesburg. *Mingary* was the name of Charles Rudd's yacht, which in its turn was named after a castle near Ardnamurchan. The yacht had a distinguished career in the First World War but it sank while rescuing survivors from the Battle of Jutland. It was later salvaged. By 1958 the marriage had become wobbly. There were many rows, and no children, which was a frustration. The crunch came when Tessa ran off with Oliver Tetley. Oliver, a few years younger than

Mingary, the house that John and Tessa built

Charles Rudd's yacht M.Y. Mingary

A crest from the menu card of M. Y. Mingary

John, had been at Eton with him, where he had seduced a maid and was known as the Eton ram. John, inspired by Oliver's green eyes, christened him 'the Green Mamba'. He had already been married twice and had two children and a reputation as a cad. Tessa had to go to Lourenço Marques in Mozambique where she had a part in a film directed by Jamie Uys. Accounts of what happened next vary. John recalls in his diary that Tessa was booked into the *Polana Hotel* and was joined by Oliver where they signed the register as *Mr and Mrs John Rudd*. John knew she was in Lourenço Marques but not that she was with Oliver. He phoned the hotel and asked for her. The Hall Porter said that she was out but that he could speak to Mr Rudd! Tessa phoned back to confess all. Her father was incensed and he and John flew up. Tessa and Oliver anticipated this and, according to the porter, set off by car, which broke down in Nelspruit, and they finished the journey by train. Dr Laubscher tracked down Oliver and informed him that if ever he saw him again he would horsewhip him. Tessa's recall is very different. It is hoped that the reader will understand that after the passage of fifty years and in all the confusion memories can be imperfect. John also received some of his information second-hand from the Hall Porter. Tessa states they travelled by train, not car. Also she is adamant that her father would never have threatened to horsewhip Oliver or ever used that expression. The marriage was effectively ended. Oliver was an interesting and intelligent man;

a cynic and a rebel; he turned against his background and fought hard against the apartheid regime. With Michael Stern he founded Waterford School, one of the first multi-racial schools in Southern Africa, where Nelson Mandela, Desmond Tutu and Walter Sisulu sent some of their children. He also helped smuggle the Tambo family out of the country. He supported the ANC and was banned from South Africa in 1961 and later lived in Swaziland. Oliver and Tessa later married and had two children, but Oliver drank and the marriage did not last. His fourth wife was Patricia Bowes Lyon, a niece of the Queen Mother. He died by his own hand in 1974. Tessa married for the third time Michael Fleischer, a German from Transylvania, whom she met at a Faschingsball, which is a German carnival. He was a talented sculptor and they were very happy.

In early 1960, De Beers sent John to Sierra Leone as a diamond buyer and he was attached to the Government Diamond Office in Kenema, the country's third city. Although he described the country as a hell hole, John enjoyed his experience there as it was the diamond business in the raw. Conditions were harsh, snakes in the bath and four inch nails in the corn cobs. The hours were long and the heat suffocating. The tour was for six months, there were six in his team and they would buy about £60,000 worth of diamonds a day. The diggers would arrive, all shapes and sizes and sometimes bare-breasted women, with the stones in a variety of wrappings – lavatory paper, aspirin tins, old envelopes – and they would haggle furiously. If a deal could not be done they would put the stones back into their hats, shirts or mouths and illegally smuggle them to Liberia where a better price might be had. But he was glad when the six months tour of duty was up and, after a short break in Europe, he could return to South Africa.

At this stage in our story it is appropriate to describe life under apartheid, the pernicious system under which all South Africans had to live. Many readers of this story will know what it was like because they lived through it. Others will know about it second-hand. But there is a generation that grew up after its abandonment and so it is best to describe for them the extraordinary business that was 'separate development' or apartheid. It was instigated by the Nationalist government when they won power in 1948. It permeated every aspect of South African life from park benches and toilets to life's fundamentals. All rights, associations and movements of the black South Africans and other minorities were curtailed by law. The law told you where you could live, whom you could marry, where you were educated, what job you could have, and how you could travel. For the blacks this was dehumanising. 3.5 million black South Africans were removed from their homes and forced into segregated neighbourhoods. In 1970, black representation was abolished and blacks were deprived of their citizenship. Apartheid set off much international resistance. As unrest spread, the state responded with repression and violence. In 1990, President de Klerk began negotiations to end it and after multi-ethnic elections in 1994, won by the African National Congress under Nelson Mandela, it finally came to an end

At the start of 1961 John was 34, a bachelor again and a well-paid business executive able to live the life of a man-about-town. In his spare time he became involved in the sponsorship and training of a number of black musical shows and operas based at *Dorkay House*, a centre for black theatre and music. This was one of the few multiracial activities tolerated by the Nationalist government. His social life involved both black and white and he would regularly drive down to the townships to meet black writers and actors. *Dorkay House* had some notable successes. They were the first to produce an Athol Fugard play and they launched Miriam Makeba. A friend, Robert Loder, recalls that they also had a good relationship with *Drum* magazine, founded by Jim Bailey, the son of the Randlord Sir Abe Bailey. John would give parties in his home in Bryanston, now a smart suburb of Johannesburg, but then a dusty new development, where both his white and black friends were invited. He was criticised for skating on thin ice but many of the whites were amazed by the quality of character as well as the colourful backgrounds of the blacks. Occasionally blacks would stay over and be driven home the next day. John was sure these activities were spied on by his neighbours and reported to the authorities One of the *Dorkay House* productions was *King Kong* when he was Chairman of the First Night Committee. They held their meetings in an opulent Johannesburg restaurant which contrasted with the run-down warehouse on the wrong side of the tracks used for rehearsals. The Nationalist government had cut off funding for the training of black doctors and the premiere was to raise money for this cause. The show had an all-black cast and chronicled the tragic life of Ezekie Dlamini, a heavyweight boxer. Miriam Makeba, who later achieved international stardom, played a Shebeen Queen. (A shebeen is an illicit drinking den). The show was a hit all over South Africa and later transferred successfully to Europe and was a remarkable flowering in the artistic desert of apartheid South Africa. The music was written by an African, Todd Matshikiza, the lyrics by a European, Pat Williams, choreography, direction and scenery were largely by Jews, the producer, Leon Gluckman was Jewish, the management European and the cast African.

The evening of Friday 19th May 1961 was to be dramatic for John. He had been working long hours in his office and on that evening left at about five o'clock to meet up with a companion, Laurie Penny, for a drink at the *Carlton Hotel* in central Johannesburg. Laurie Penny was a good friend of John's who never failed to amuse him. He stuck with him and always was a help in the following tribulations. Sadly he was to die in an accident by falling off a ladder. They moved on to a nightclub in Marshall Street where John had arranged for some cabaret artists to audition for the management. A dancer, Dorothy Tiyo, and her boyfriend Clement were to be there but they did not arrive. In one of his diaries John records how he first met Dottie, as she was known to everyone. At work he felt his talents were not being fully stretched. Indeed, he felt he was just a wage-slave for the Oppenheimers. An opportunity for promotion had come up when a colleague had had a nervous breakdown but he had been passed over. There currently was no romance in his life and the gloomy political situation was getting him down; he felt in need of some stimulating friendships. He first saw her on stage and he was immediately impressed by her sparkling personality. Afterwards a mutual friend, John King, introduced them. She was wearing a big green jersey, brown slacks and a pondock* on her head. John mentioned that they had many friends in common in the cast of *King Kong*. 'Oh. You are John Rudd. I've heard much about you' she replied, and they chatted away. Soon she was being invited to parties at John's house and he was touring the township shebeens with her, where she showed him three bullet scars on her legs which she had received in the 1956 New Brighton riots in Port Elizabeth.

For much of 1961 and 1962 Dottie was the darling of *Drum* magazine. There were frequent articles about her containing light-hearted gossip and many photos, including a dramatic one of her on the cover. For a while she was their agony aunt. The June 1961 edition had a four page article about her

* The authors have been unable to discover exactly what a pondock is, but it must be a hat.

Dottie as portrayed in the Johannesburg Post newspaper in 1962

in Damon Runyon style, illustrated with eight pictures, written by Casey Motsisi, one of *Drum's* celebrated writers. Here is an edited extract:

'The first time I met Dottie Tiyo – she was then currently Miss South Africa – she was a curvy girl weighing around 120lbs. the curves are still there, but the weight has been knocked out for a home-run. In fact you can describe her as the Zsa Zsa Gabor of the Reef as lean. And she was beautiful. Maybe today

she has lost some fresh loveliness, but boy! Has she gained in zing since then? Said a guy who knows Dottie: 'Dottie has stretched every hour of the day and night into two hours. And you can't live the way Dottie does 48 hours a day, and still expect to be on top form!'

Dottie says she left Port Elizabeth with the sole intention of becoming a stage star and a model. She had little or no training in both fields, but the girl was determined. Clutching a frugal wardrobe and £25 in cash, she hopped on a train for the Golden City. That was in June 1959. With the help of such veterans like Hazel Futa and Dolly Rathebe, she quickly learnt the ways of the city. Modelling offers poured in. She was mostly seen at Dorkay House, where Union Artists have their office, being coached in singing. Before long she was one of the chorus girls in the King Kong jazz opera. Her face graced magazine covers. The girl was becoming famous, to be sure. And this in a six months of her arrival.

Since then she has toured the Union with African Jazz, living it up and generally enjoying herself.

An incident that will forever remain vivid in my mind is about the night we were from a party with some friends and Dottie. We were all thoroughly pickled. The driver had made arrangements to drop each one off at his place. Dottie was sleeping it off on another guy's shoulder in the back of the car. He too was as tight as a miser's fist. When we arrived at this guy's place, he could not get out in time. He was that tight. His wife came out of the house to see what was happening; she was not pleased. She saw Dottie; she got mad.

'Who are you?' Dottie demanded.

'This is my husband,' said the comely wife.

'So what?' Dottie wanted to know. Then all hell broke loose. Just to show her 'so what' the wife retraced her steps to the house. She came back holding something that looked like a snake in her right hand. Without saying a word she hauled Dottie out of the Volksie and lashed away at her with the sjambok. What a racket! When Dottie could not take any more, she did the next best thing. She bolted like a startled deer, leaving one of her sandals behind, in her quest for safer horizons. The woman picked it up. I volunteered to take it back to Dottie. 'Let her come and fetch it herself, if she wants it, the .....' The husband and shoe were dragged into the house. To this day the woman refuses to go to any of Dottie's shows. 'I think I will lose my temper to such

an extent that I will go on the stage and scratch her eyes out in front of all those people. I'm not through with her yet. Even if I met her in Eloff Street I'm going to hit her on the head with a bottle full of sand.' I told this to Dottie and pleaded with her to watch her step. Although I like watching fights – inside and outside the ring – this one is a fight in which I will do a Dag Hammarskjold and ask the warring females of the species to disarm

'But why do you never leave other people's husbands alone, Dottie?' I asked her.

'They also take my boyfriends. And I don't complain. Fair's fair'.

Dottie has no relations in Jossie, but that couldn't stop her from leaving her parents in Port Elizabeth and coming up here all by her little self. PE apparently wasn't her piece of pie. Besides she has seen some of the guys in King Kong when the show was down there, and that settled her mind to come over yonder.

The first person she stayed with was Lefty Maruping in Dube. But that was not for long. For some reason or other the Marupings decided that having two women under one roof was not healthy. They politely asked her to make other arrangements. This decision sparked off a chain reaction of similar incidents which is still continuing. Even today Dottie has no permanent place to stay. She's everybody's next-door neighbour. From Maruping she went to Thandeka Mpampani's home with her troubles. She took her under her wing. But not for long. Then to prittiful King Konger, Mumsie Mthombeni's place. Then to another guy in Dube. Then to a certain Florence in Killarney, a suburb in town. Then to ….. ag, we could go on like this until next year.

Not so long ago I was looking at posters. And who should happen along with Bonny Molantoa but The Dot!

'Casey, meet my new boyfriend,' Dottie cooed with the light shining brightly in her eyes. I called Dottie aside.

'But that guy in Western you said you wanted to marry, what about him?'

'Oh, I left him last week.'

'But he and Bonny are best friends,' I pointed out.

'I know that. That way they won't fight each other over me over me.' I was beat. My advice to you girls: Hang onto your boyfriends when Dottie's around. Said Can Themba of Dottie: 'After you have been kissed by Dottie Tiyo when she exudes passion, you will need to be unplastered off her.'

I was at the rehearsals of the Drums of Africa show in which Dottie does her near-nude snake dance when Alf Herbert came up to me and asked what I was doing there talking to Dottie. I told him. He said, 'If you wrote the true story of Dottie you wouldn't get it published.' Dottie's snake dance is controversial. Some like it, others don't. The Star wrote about it, 'The temptation dance by Dottie Tiyo in the tribal scene was quite something. It made me feel minute.'

I asked Dottie why she was left out of King Kong when it went to London. 'I did not want to go' she said. That one was suspect. I rang a highly-placed official of the Union Artists executive and put the question to him. 'Well, er, I don't think we wanted her to go along. But to be fair to Dottie, I don't think she was keen to go.' All the same London should be happy she was spared Dottie. That kid would have set the place on fire ...and not with her acting ability either. That kid! She swears her new love, Clement, of the Midnite Kids, is the only guy who has succeeded in making her turn over a new leaf.

FOOTNOTE: I asked Dottie to read this piece and sign it. She signed it without reading it. 'Read it and tell me if it's okay.' I pleaded with her. 'I don't care what you say about me as long as the spelling of my name is correct,' she answered.'

Dottie's comment on the spelling of her name is ironic. The press often got it wrong and John always spelt it wrongly, writing Dotty. The article is a good example of the bravura journalism for which *Drum* became well known, but no doubt the picture it paints is highly coloured to fit her stage persona rather than the real girl at home.

Can Themba is mentioned in the article. He became a good friend of John's and was one of the most celebrated of the *Drum* writers. One of his best known stories was *From the Bottom of a Bottle* - a phrase he took too seriously. Indeed he lived up to the slogan of the *Drum* press room, 'Live fast, die young and have a good-looking corpse.' Can was banned by the apartheid authorities, which meant it was illegal even to read his writings. He died in exile in Swaziland at the age of 43. He wrote to John in 1960 saying, 'I would like to finish my book *To Hell With It!* but it interferes with my drinking'.

John was to write of Dottie, 'She is much deeper than just a snake dancer. Born in Port Elizabeth, her father was arrested in the Treason Trials, she made her own way to Johannesburg and by her own quick wits, vitality and

AFRICAN FIREBALL—

Here is sizzling Dotty

DOTTY IN HER SNAKE DANCE

THERE are two Dotty Tiyos. One is the 21-year-old beauty queen, whose romances and ructions are regular as sundown, who does the most electrifying "sizzle" and "snake" dances in any night-club in South Africa.

The other is the Dotty who, just as regularly, comes shatteringly up against the fact that her skin is the wrong colour, and that a black girl must only be gay according to the South African laws.

Both Dotties made headlines last week when she and ex-Guards officer Bevil Rudd, white grandson of a diamond mining king, were sentenced to six months' imprisonment. They were found guilty under South Africa's Immorality Act which forbids sexual relations between white and black. They have been freed pending an appeal.

Top model

To black Africans, Dotty is *the* symbol of the girl who doesn't care, who burns the candle at both ends and then douses it in a glass of champagne.

The last of a family of 11, she was seven when her mother died. Eleven years later, she burst into Johannesburg with nothing but hope and energy to offer.

Soon she was a top model, a cover girl, a jazz singer and a knock-out chorine in the African musical "King Kong."

And meanwhile, the legend grew. Dotty helped it.

"If you want to find me, don't look for me among girls, brother." . . . "I can get all the things marriage offers without getting married." . . . "I don't care what you say about me as long as the spelling of my name's correct." . . .

It was while Dotty was in the South African production of "King Kong" that Bevil Rudd went to audition her for the London production.

That night, Rudd went drinking with Dotty, whose friends say: "She can drink 'em faster than you can pour 'em."

In court, the prosecution alleged they were found in Rudd's house early next morning, Rudd wearing only a towel and Dotty hiding in a cupboard, wearing only Rudd's yellow dressing-gown.

Dottie in her Snake Dance from The News of the World

personality soon made a name for herself throughout the country. Her verve and spirit blazed a path and overnight she became a symbol to thousands in the townships of a girl whom nothing can keep down'.

John and Laurie Penny then went to the *York Hotel* in search of a meal but the restaurant had closed and John was tired after a hard week and needed a pick-me-up, so they made do with several beers and brandies. The next port of call was *Ghandi Hall* in Fox Street to see a play, *A View from the Bridge* by Arthur Miller. They arrived after the interval, Lorimer's girlfriend joined them and after the show they went on to the *Canton* restaurant for dinner, but for the second time they were unlucky as it was closing. They were joined by two journalists, Joe Lowe and Richard Oakshott. Richard was a quixotic figure. While at University he had gone to help the Hungarian revolutionaries and later been made a Hero of the Revolution. Subsequently he was Paris correspondent of the *Financial Times*. The plan was to show him some real South African life. The party went on to the *Stirling Hotel* where more brandies were consumed. Eventually they found food at the *Crescent* restaurant in Fordsburg, which was washed down by more brandies. John then announced that he had to go to Sophiatown in search of a couple of artistes. Sophiatown was a black suburb well known for its bohemian and artistic lifestyle. A few years later it was systematically destroyed by the Nationalist government, the inhabitants removed, and a new white suburb built called *Triomf,* Afrikaans for triumph. After the fall of apartheid it was rechristened Sophiatown. On arrival John picked up Dottie and a friend of hers, Gladys, and drove them off to the nightclub for the audition, but the proprietor was leaving so it was rearranged for another night. The party moved on to the *Carlton Hotel*, then the *Langham*, then back to the Municipal Market in Sophiatown in search of minestrone soup, and finally back to the *Crescent* restaurant where they drank a bottle of brandy mixed with a peppermint cordial. The next stop was a house in the suburb of Dube, the home of George Nhlapo, where more brandy and beer were provided. It was hoped that George could put Dottie and Gladys up for the night but all his accommodation was taken up by his family, so John set off to his home in Bryanston with the two girls, a journey that was illegal in South Africa at the time. On arrival he pointed to a bedroom for the girls in the attic, collapsed into his bed in his underpants and fell into a deep sleep.

At 8.45 the next morning, with a mother-and-father of a hangover, he was awakened by banging at the door and the window and, much to his astonishment, Dottie was lying naked in the bed beside him. He tried unsuccessfully to wake her up and then went to the window, drew the curtain and, to his amazement, saw a uniformed police officer gesticulating to him to open up. He redrew the curtain, with difficulty aroused Dottie, dressed her in one of his blue shirts and a yellow towel, picked up her clothes which were scattered around the room, put her shoes neatly in a cupboard, her jacket on a hanger and her panties under his pillow. Then he took hold of Dottie, told her to keep down so the police would not see her, and pushed her into a cupboard in the bathroom and covered her with dirty clothes. Thinking this cupboard perhaps unsuitable, particularly as the police might prod the laundry pile with a bayonet, he removed her and placed her in another higher one which contained suitcases, out of which she fell, bringing the door down with her and breaking a table. He then pushed her into an umbrella cupboard by the bedroom door. In retrospect he recalled that this was not a wise move. When the police opened the laundry cupboard he saw that she would not have been detected. Her wraith-like figure, perfected by much snake dancing, made her malleable and flexible and so a good fit. Finally John opened the door to the police and Inspector Stephens and Detective Sergeant Terblanche and other officers came in. Stephens said, 'We have reason to suspect there is a Bantu woman in here with you.' And he quoted the Immorality Act which had been enacted in 1927 and provided a term of imprisonment of up to seven years for sexual relations across the racial divide. It came out later that a certain Mr Abrahams had called the police. He must have been a neighbour of John's and when the merry party arrived at about 4 o'clock in the morning he would have been disturbed, seen that they were of different races, and made his phone call. John told Stephens there was no Bantu woman there and the policemen started their search. Eventually he found Dottie's cupboard and shouted, 'Kom uit. Kom uit,' ('Come out, Come out' in English) and out she came. Sergeant Terblanche was beside himself with excitement and John noticed his nostrils quiver, observing the hatred the Afrikaners had for the English. Stephens said, 'This, in case you did not know, is illegal' and John noticed that one of the officers was Sergeant Duvenhage, to whom he had given a kipper supper after a *King Kong* performance. John was allowed to shave, took three Alka-Seltzers, and phoned his office and David Schneider, his lawyer. He also informed his captors he proposed to phone Jackie Kennedy, the wife of the US President. In fact he tried the US Ambassador but, it being Saturday morning, he could not get through.

The two of them were bundled into a police Volkswagen and driven down to Ferndale Police Station. This in fact was not John's first clash with Afrikaner justice. Some years earlier he was in a nightclub in an old church down in the Cape Town docks. A skirmish broke out. The police came and, with truncheons flailing, manhandled the apparent victim off the premises. John, a witness, was outraged by this treatment and vehemently expressed his views to the police, who responded by bundling him into the back of one of their wagons. He spent the night in the cells and was released without charge the next morning. Once in the station, John and Dottie were separated, and John was left in an office where he drank quantities of water from a terracotta jug. When describing these events in his diary, John, for the first of a number of times, records that, as 'nothing happened', he was confident that the charges would be dropped. He was unaware that he was vulnerable to both a charge of committing an 'immoral act' and also conspiring to commit one. David Schneider arrived and then he and John were driven to the District Surgeon's office. The lugubrious Dr Bukhoper called John in and asked him to strip. His pubic hairs were examined and John was pleased to note that no Xhosa curls were found there. Then his eyes, nose and ears were checked and swabs taken. Then, along with David, the two of them, Dottie still in the yellow robe, rushed to the Magistrates' Court to arrange bail before it closed at midday. They were remanded until June 5th and David, who was an outstanding support throughout the whole process, drove them back to John's house, *Mingary*. Dottie was at last reunited with her clothes and she spent the rest of the afternoon playing gramophone records and reading John's books. That evening John drove her home. She sat in the front of the car reading poetry. John told her that he was hopeful the whole thing would be dropped as, after all, 'absolutely nothing happened.' They filled up with petrol at a garage and a car load of Africans waved at them and said that is the way the country ought to be.

On the following Monday morning, John went to his office while apprehensively looking at the papers to see if there were any press reports.

The two accused

This is Dottie Tiyo, the young Xhosa dancer who is charged with Bevil John Blyth Rudd with an offence under the Immorality Act. Well known as an entertainer, Dottie Tiyo is a former non-European beauty queen, and recently acted in "Tremor," a multi-racial film produced on the Rand

BEVIL JOHN RUDD

John and Dottie after their arrest in the Johannesburg Sunday Times

His first call was to the Public Relations department where he used to work to brief them and to see if the saga could be kept out of the papers. Lloyd Williams, the head, told him this was impossible. John returned to his desk and tore up a diary he had been keeping. Then a colleague showed him the midday edition of *The Star* where, on page three, there was a four inch column report. Robin, John's brother, who worked in the same office, then came to join him. Robin had married Alison Maclean, whose nephew is the actor Hugh Grant.

John noticed that most of his work colleagues gave him cold, reserved looks and the two of them decided it was best to leave, which they did via the back entrance. Harry Oppenheimer was supportive. He invited John to dinner at his home, Brenthurst, and offered financial help. Harry's wife Bridget was more critical. When it was remarked that John might have to go and work in Japan, she quipped "Why not go to China? It is further". Harry also indicated that John's job was secure but that he might have to work away from South Africa for a while. John wrote that he felt that he was in the Headmaster's study after some terrible misdemeanour. John had adopted the role of Court Jester at the court of King Harry and was always welcome there, but this relationship led to resentment from other executives. Julian Ogilvie Thompson, later Chairman of Anglo American, found John exasperating.

For most of the next few weeks John would be busy in David Schneider's office preparing his defence. He was still confident the matter would be dropped, but as the days went by, and it was not, this confidence waned. At the same time he became more determined to stand by Dottie, fight the charges and also the injustices from which they arose.

The trial of John and Dottie began on July 7th 1961 and was a national and international sensation. The court was packed with their supporters, described by the press as white debutantes and socialites, and such was the commotion that the magistrate, Mr Owen Gush, who was Chief Magistrate of South Africa, warned that if there was any disturbance he would clear the gallery. John's mother Ursula was also there. She had since remarried and was now Mrs Wally Machel. Some of the family thought she had married beneath her but she had been left short of money as a widow and fortunately Wally had a few bob. In fact he was a great support. He had made his money as a hay merchant at Smithfield and talked with a cockney accent.

John's defence counsel, Cecil Margo, had a formidable task for, while there was no direct evidence of the 'offence', the circumstantial evidence was considerable. Margo was a distinguished advocate who had served in the South African Air Force in the war, winning the DFC and DSO, but criminal cases were not his speciality. Before the case came to court he had had a meeting with the South African Attorney General, Rudy Reis, where he had argued that the Immorality Acts were in conflict with Human Rights legislation to which South Africa had signed up. Reis was sympathetic but rejected this argument, pointing out that certain states in the US had laws against miscegenation which, in fact, were not repealed until 1967. Dottie was separately represented and chose not to testify. This counted against the two of them as many in the court would have liked to ask her the question, 'What were you doing naked in John's bed?'

In his opening remarks Margo stated that the law required conclusive evidence of an immoral act and noted that the prosecutor, Mr. Landin, had included an alternative charge of conspiracy to perform an immoral act. The prosecutor's case rested on these six points:

- That both the accused were in a state of undress.
- That each side of the double bed had been slept in.
- That Dottie and her friend Gladys were in Rudd's house until the early hours of the morning.
- That the police knocked for 25 minutes until they were admitted.
- That each of the accused gave naïve and untruthful explanations for their predicament.
- That Dottie was wearing John's clothes.

Margo pointed out that John intended the two girls to sleep in the attic or the annex in the stables and underlined the fact that there was no evidence that they had gone to bed together. The reason Dottie did not go to the attic was because she was too tipsy to negotiate the ladder. However all his endeavours were in vain. There was frenetic activity around the court on the morning judgement was to be given. Outside, cameras flashed and whirled and inside, every space was taken; John was not confident but he hoped for perhaps a suspended sentence. All along, his advisors had told him to remain detached from Dottie so that observers would think there was no special rapport between them, but such was his loyalty to her that he ignored this. Throughout the hearings Gush had brought along some guests to witness the proceedings who sat on the police benches. There was one woman whose face John described as 'serious and repulsive'. Gush would have foretold to her the result and, as soon as she walked in and John saw her expression, he realised the game was up. Gush took a long time in his pronouncement and eventually came round to announcing a guilty verdict and a six months sentence each. John noticed a row of Police Sergeants, crop-haired Gestapo types, who had kept their piercing eyes on him all morning, jump in the air with glee at the announcement. The two of them were sent down to the cells while Margo sought leave to appeal and applied for bail. Then Dottie burst into tears and Tatu, John's first wife's sister, came down to cheer her up. Leave to appeal was given and bail granted and John was keen for him and Dottie to leave the

A police photo of the photographer's assistant illustrating the attic stairs which Dottie was unable to negotiate

court together, but his lawyers and friends were unanimously against this and in the end Tatu escorted Dottie out. David Veitch, another of John's friends, drove John in his Volkswagen to the Laubscher home, Gale House, for lunch and Dottie arrived with Tatu. John's next appointment was at Brenthurst in Harry Oppenheimer's yellow study where, over whisky and soda, Harry was very supportive and it was arranged that, while he waited for the appeal, John was to write a short biography of Sir Ernest. John then went home to *Mingary* where Letty the maid told him the press had been staked out all day, hiding in the bushes and loitering in the drive, but luckily the last one had just left. Then he, along with David Veitch, drove Dottie to Durban to stay in Mrs Phillips' boarding house. At intersections they put a blanket over her head. They arrived back at 4 am in time for David to attend a board meeting with a group of fruit importers. But Dottie was not happy in Durban and after a few days, weeping, she called John, pleading to come back to Johannesburg. She flew up and, to a background of flashing press photographers, John and Tatu greeted her. Dottie was in a grumpy mood as she thought John was not pleased that she had come back. The room in her lodgings in Sophiatown was not available so, while John stayed at David Veitch's, she stayed at *Mingary* for a night or two while new lodgings were found. She and Clement were meant to go on tour arranged by the impresario Wally Herbert, but they opted out. This was a lucky escape as the tour bus crashed down a hillside, injuring a number of the performers. It should be mentioned that, although he was a boyfriend of Dottie and also her dancing partner, he lived up to his name and, while John was romancing Dottie, he never caused any trouble and all the time was extremely helpful. Tessa and her new husband then appeared on the scene from Swaziland, from where they had kept in touch with John and followed the trial. Although Oliver had offered to organise an escape for John, he preferred to stay and face the music. John sensed things were not too good between them. They had read much about the case in the English papers and wanted to meet Dottie. Oliver and John set off to see her in her new lodgings. They were sitting in her room drinking wine by candlelight when Clement, mildly under the influence of marijuana, called in and then a police car drew up outside, no doubt attracted by the large Mercedes parked outside at midnight. Clement went out to meet the officers with a view to drawing them away from John and Oliver, but then Oliver decided to talk his way out of the situation and John joined him. 'What the hell are you doing here?' demanded an officer. John responded by jumping into the back of their car, slamming the door so hard that he considered he had damaged it, and saying, 'Take me to your police station'. The officers tried to pull him out but he would not budge so, as he recalled, with gold buttons, vicious faces, khaki mackintoshes, revolvers and much polished leather they got into the car with him. 'The master race has got me again', he mused, but in fact they just decided to take his name and address and, after a few abusive words directed at Clement, got him out and drove away. John then went into the house to say goodbye to Dottie when a great commotion broke out. Oliver was driving off and then Clement shouted, 'Run'. John went out of the window into the back yard. Dottie tried to contact Oliver and the car. Police, neighbours and residents were running in every direction. John managed to get into the car and off they sped to Bryanston with police car lights flashing in the distance behind them. Tessa was horrified

Laurie Penny spiriting Dottie away from court

Currie's

PROPERTY AUCTIONS

SALE OF

Attractive Bryanston Home

LOT 82 WITKOPPEN ROAD

FAVOURED WITH INSTRUCTIONS FROM JOHN RUDD, ESQ.

At Our Mart, "Auction House," 111, Fox Street

THURSDAY, 7th SEPTEMBER, 1961

AT 11 A.M.

A home with great unconventional charm offering infinite possibilities. Excellent position, within walking distance of shopping centre and school, property comprises 3 acres of easy to care for indigenous wooded and secluded garden, now showing to full advantage the many flowering shrubs. Custom-built, using best materials throughout, designed by a leading architect, and all in excellent taste. The part double-storey home under Brozeley tiles, faces North and stands away from road.

Downstairs are very large lounge of unusual character with recessed fireplace and picture windows, ideal in every way for entertaining, and with French doors to brick-paved patio, dining-room, cloakroom and beautiful luxurious bedroom suite with fitted dressing-room, colour tiled bathroom with sunken bath, louvre windows and doors to garden.

Up ladder staircase is second spacious double bedroom with fine view and hot and cold water laid on.

Modern fitted kitchen has natural wood finish.

The servants' rooms and bathroom are of particularly attractive appearance with thatched roof, and there is a fine pool of rustic design (unfiltered).

Also in garden is a quaint weekend cottage with bath.

Bond to approved purchaser.

Full details from the Auctioneers, phone 34-3331. (After hours phone Bryanston 81 or 271 – dial 47)

RICHARD R. CURRIE (PTY.) LTD. Premier

Auctioneers, Estate Agents and Sworn Appraisers
BLOODSTOCK SALESMEN

"AUCTION HOUSE," 111 FOX STREET, JOHANNESBURG

BOX 614 Telegraphic Add.: "PROMPT" PHONE 34-3331

The advertisement for the sale of Mingary

when she discovered what her husband and ex-husband had got up to. Oliver was vulnerable to deportation and John's attitude to the police that night was that they could do what they liked to him.

Looking back on the case and taking into account all the evidence from John's diaries when he records 'nothing happened', it is clear that they were innocent of the charge, indeed of both charges, for they had not planned for anything to happen either. But there is an earlier entry in the diaries where John indicates that on at least one occasion he knew Dottie very well indeed. So, ironically, while they did not commit the offences for which they were tried, they did do so on another occasion and were not tried.

Between the court hearing and the hearing of the appeal John and Dottie remained in close contact. Some of John's letters survive which, had they fallen into the wrong hands, would have scuppered their case for good. As a precaution they were sent via third parties. Those for John were sent to Mrs Todd, his secretary. He wrote in one, 'Tonight I kept getting the feeling I've never loved anyone so much as you ever in my life'. John often travelled up to Port Elizabeth, where Dottie's family lived, to see her. She was the youngest of eleven children and her mother had died when she was seven. To add an extra dimension, her father was the local African National Congress leader and whenever John visited he was conscious of the police hovering around.

In spite of the spectre of jail on the horizon, John was often in party mood; probably this was escapism or defiance. A few days after these dramas, he took Oliver, Tessa and Dottie to the house of a bohemian friend known as Ruth St. M. in Highlands North. They were met with rum, drums and wine. John felt things needed livening up and danced the Drum dance with Dottie. This was all too much for Oliver, who wanted to leave, but then he caught the mood and stayed on. It struck John that he should not be seen with Dottie in public but then he thought he was probably safe in Ruth's large, well-timbered suburban house.

John's legal costs were such that he had to sell his house. He decided the least painful method was by auction and he put it in the hands of *Curries*. A large advertisement was placed in the papers and an open day was arranged for the public one Sunday. About 700 people came; they trampled over everything, stole two Alsatian puppies and asked Letty, the maid, if she was Dottie. The double bed was of great interest to them. John thought of setting the police after the stolen puppies but feared the publicity might be unfavourable.

John's next move was to fly down to Cape Town to visit his ageing grandfather, who was resting in his bed in his seaside house in St. James. It was a nostalgic trip and, as a 20 year old, he had run along the beach where he had spent the last summer with his father. The sight of the prison on Robben Island was ominous. He found the old man surrounded by lights, bells, wirelesses and magnifying glasses and chatted away to him about the old times with Rhodes, Sir Ernest and Kimberley. Percy was surprised to hear that Harry Oppenheimer planned to keep John working for him and he did not criticise John's behaviour at all. As John left, he felt he would not see Percy again. He next called on Tatu, Tessa's sister, a student at Cape Town University. At the *Mount Nelson Hotel* they met with Randolph Vigne and Sheila Camerer. She was then Miss Cape Town University and was later to become a human rights lawyer, a Nationalist MP, a Democratic Alliance MP and finally South African ambassador to Bulgaria. John and Tatu moved on to the *Café Royal* and then to a club called *Naughton's Den* for Spanish dancing. Finally, John drove round Sea Point to drop her off at her Uncle De Villiers' house and, as they swept around the headland, she insisted on sitting on the fender of the car. They drove down to Hout Bay for a swim and the car stuck in the sand, so they walked back to the fishing village for help. Tatu tripped on a piece of submerged boat in the sand and damaged her foot, so John carried her. There was no help to be found in the village, just a strong smell of fish, so they decided to wait until dawn and climbed through a window and went to sleep in a truck. At sunrise, the fishermen arrived and they went in search of the car. It could not be found and John feared it had gone out to sea, a cause for concern as it was not his. Then a four-wheeled police truck arrived. A fisherman had alerted them that the factory had been broken into. John thought the police had come to help and was surprised when he was arrested. He tried to talk his way out of the situation, using the car, now found, and Tatu's foot as evidence. It was explained that she had a French exam at the university at 9 o'clock. Eventually an obliging police officer drove her there. Back at the fish factory, John paid £2 to the owner for some large sheets of paper that they had used for warmth and he was let off after names and addresses were taken. Half-full of sand, the car was returned to its owner and he breakfasted at the *Mount Nelson* and watched one of those glorious Cape Town winter mornings with the mountain lit up by the sun and the mist rising slowly from the town and the docks. He flew back to Johannesburg that morning.

Ciro's nightclub wanted Dottie to do a show for them. John negotiated a fee of £50 for two nights. She had had no work since their arrest and also it was illegal for her to appear in front of an all-white audience, but he particularly wanted her to do it as he felt it would do the stuffy whites good to see her explosive talent. During the rehearsals they would meet up afterwards at Ruth's house. She told him that Dottie was getting very fond of him and she wanted to know if John was in love with her. John sketches in his diary a colourful picture of Ruth. He describes her as a mournful, pretty lady with big eyes. She ran a school for African models which was always closing down and then reopening, and she also made costumes for the theatre. She had been married once before and was reputed to be a lesbian for half the year. Now she was married to a small, gnarled, taciturn fellow who was a shop decorator. She ran an old Renault car that never worked. The house, old and large, was dilapidated, with dogs and cats wandering in and out. Shady African jazz musicians were to be found in the back rooms, which were made of tin. Ruth was very kind and often lent Dottie a bed when she was in town.

John could not keep away from the police for long. There was the incident when he took Dottie to his dentist. There was a lot of work to be done and she was given gas. The dental nurse disapproved of her being there and sent her home before she came round properly. Out in the street she was staggering around, bumping into bicycles and parked cars. Much to the astonishment of onlookers, John took her by the arm and escorted her to David Vietch's nearby flat. He had no key and entered by the bathroom window. A journalist friend, John Goldblatt, came round and he then drove her home to 42 Letaba Street, calling in on the police station on the way for her to sign the bail book. They had no permit to be driving in a black area so, as a precaution, he planned to drop her off at the bus station, a few blocks from her home. But they were out of luck; a cream-colored Volkswagen drew up behind and out jumped a policeman and a CID officer who asked for their permits. John persuaded them, in view of Dottie's operation, to allow him to drop her home and, when he got back to the station, a Captain Petit had arrived who announced that John had been seen dropping off Dottie the previous night 'Why did you kiss her goodnight?' he asked menacingly. John, extraordinarily, had forgotten about this, but in fact they had been having dinner at an Indian dancing show with a friend called Bey and had been chased by a pick-up van which they had lost at an intersection. Bey thought the police were going to shoot and said it was the most exciting moment of his life. Anyhow, the Captain charged them and told them to come to court in the morning. John Goldblatt was worried as he thought he might be deported and damage his career. As it was, David Schneider, John's lawyer, sorted it out and they were fined £1 but not before *The Star* newspaper picked up the story, reporting 'Rudd fined for being in township'. John was becoming tired of all this agitation and was considering abandoning the appeal and facing the music. He drove off to Swaziland to a hideout in the Mbabane Valley and by candlelight drafted a possible surrender declaration. On his return he cleared it with Dottie.

Next came Dottie's appearance at *Ciro's*. John thought it better not to be at the club but waited at Gale House, keeping in touch by telephone. Then he repaired to Ruth's house to await the return of Dottie and her entourage, but by two in the morning they were not back and he returned to *Mingary*. Then the calls started coming through saying the performance was a triumph. For the next performance he did go and hid in a small changing room drinking red champagne. He set off for Ruth's ahead of the others but the post-show party was an anti-climax. There had been bomb threats to *Ciro's* and he had a scene with Dottie about nothing. On reflection he was glad the shows had gone ahead and that they had crashed the colour bar again and he hoped the publicity had been helpful.

With a view to the further promotion of Dottie's career John introduced her to the Spanish Consul. She came round to his flat and then collapsed on the sofa in terrible pain. He took her home and heard the next day that she had been admitted to the Coronation Hospital. He went round there and found her condition was mystifying the medics – there was talk of Fallopian tubes and appendixes. The doctor in charge decided to operate immediately and, given that it was a hospital for blacks, John was impressed by the high standard of staff and equipment. He fetched some flowers and then the doctor allowed him to wait in his changing room. After three quarters of an hour the doctor returned and announced it was a straightforward appendix and that all was well. When she came round, the black Sisters surrounded her with a wall of screens and allowed John to sit at the bedside. The press had got wind of the drama and photographers had tried to get into the hospital but were blocked by the Sisters. Soon Dottie was sitting up in a blue top shirt and white scarf and she giggled as she gripped John's hand while she drifted in and out of consciousness. Then a white matron arrived and removed the screens. John noted she was about 45 and quite attractive, and he got the impression she thought he should not be in a native hospital on a women's ward after visiting hours. He left quietly and had dinner at Gale House where he would have liked to unburden himself, but there was nobody suitable he could talk to.

That Sunday, the film *Tremor*, in which Dottie had a part, was shown to a preview audience. John donned dark glasses, thinking they would give him anonymity, and went with a friend who he kept close behind. This subterfuge was short lived as Gordon Winter, the journalist from *The Sunday Express,* sat next to them. Luckily he was a friend of John's and agreed to keep quiet and sent his photographer away. Dottie played the good-time girlfriend of a boxer and John thought she was excellent.

John visited the hospital on the next two days and the press harassment continued. On the first day he was called in and asked by the doctor just to call during visiting hours. He replied that the two of them had to have discussions about the legal arrangements. He was surprised to read a colourful version of this conversation in the *Vanderland* newspaper the next day. On the Tuesday, as he approached the hospital he noticed a grey Opel driving slowly towards him with two Europeans inside. As it approached, a flash light went off and John protected his face with his briefcase. He then drove round to the other side of the hospital and entered through a window. The photographers were following so he put on a white coat and then got on a stretcher and asked two orderlies to wheel him to the lifts. Once inside, he met Clement and they chatted away, and he left clothes and magazines for Dottie.

On the next Sunday, he was driving with Letty to *Mingary* to pick up some effects when a crimson Dauphine car rammed into their side and the woman driver fell out, quite badly injured, into the road. A large crowd arrived and then the police appeared who were more interested in the crowd than the woman. An ambulance took her away and the police drew their revolvers to disperse the crowd. John picked up her property and then went to her address to inform her relations. He met her son–in-law and discovered that she was quite accident prone and he was used to such happenings. The *Rand Daily Mail* got hold of the story and incorrectly reported that Laurie Penny was in the car. When the amazed Lorrie read it he thought John had Dottie with him under a blanket and had just given his name. Such were the complexities of travel in apartheid South Africa.

The next day, Dottie left the hospital, spent the night at Ruth's, and in the morning flew to Port Elizabeth. John and a friend, Daphne, accompanied her to the airport and John took his car to the side of the terminal to wave to her as she boarded. A policeman noticed him and alerted others. John drove to the car park and hid. Uniformed and plain clothes policemen together with airline officials poured out of the terminal to search for him. He kept low and they temporarily gave up. Then he pretended to open the boot and out they swarmed again. Daphne came out and he quickly scooped her up pointing out all the attention they had generated, and drove off.

Robin, John's brother, came round to John's flat later that day to report that Percy had died. All the relatives flew down to the Cape and made the *Mount Nelson Hotel* their headquarters. Although John was not to receive anything directly from the will, Percy's death meant that a Trust fell in and, with the agreement of cousins, he would have a certain amount of capital. Both John and his brother thought much of their father at this time and John looked back on Percy's life. He had been fond of John and always trusted him but in later years he had led a selfish existence, devoted basically to his own immediate comfort, and his hostility to Ursula, John's mother, was inexcusable. On the day of the funeral, at Robin's suggestion, John placed a bet on a horse running number five, Percy's favourite number. John was new to funerals and was one of the pallbearers, a task that gave him 'ghastly shivers'. Harry Oppenheimer attended and John was grateful for his support. It was a cold winter's day but the sun shone and as they left Kalk Bay church for the cemetery they passed Rhodes's cottage, *Rocklands*. At the weekend John visited the grave alone and then headed north to grapple with the challenges there.

First he flew to Port Elizabeth under an assumed name. He checked into a run-down hotel up on the hill and that evening an exuberant Dottie, totally recovered from the operation, arrived with her sister and an ex-boyfriend. She announced she was going to jail for the man she loved and they chatted light-heartedly about their fate. The following day John met Dottie's stepmother and aunt and he explained all the legal complications of the situation. Dottie said she was all set for jail. It was not new to her. She had spent a night there for a Pass Law offence but she was apprehensive about the cold showers and food. All this made John feel better and he was heartened by a piece in *The Post* where Dottie's father was quoted as saying, 'John is a man'.

After leaving her and while still in Port Elizabeth John wrote Dottie a letter. It went:

'I feel very happy tonight. It did seem very risky coming here. What you said about jail has been a great help to me. You made me very happy having decided you loved me, and also that you wanted to go to jail. Remember they have only imprisoned your body and not your spirit. I will think of you and I have been unable not to do so since that first night we met in the De Beers café. David will have to come a lot, one day to you and then to me so we can get reports. We certainly have some wonderful memories of Verwoerd's wonderful regime. Remember the night we finally found each other, the party on that corner, the gin you stole, the Tshombe dinner, the candle-lit night at No 8.

Sorry to not have written from the Cape. Actually I was very shocked by Grandfather's death, being 92 he seemed indestructible. He helped me a lot and he was a bit of history – born before diamonds were discovered and being Rhodes' friend. At the funeral I thought most of you – in the blazing sun and the southeaster wind and the mountains in the distance as the coffin was lowered. I stood to attention in great respect to the old man and the era that was ending with him. Do see that these letters are buried or destroyed. If they ever get into the wrong hands it would be serious and we have both had enough of brute force for 1961.'

John did not follow his own advice and kept a copy of this letter in his files.

On the plane back he sat next to a large Afrikaner woman who was reading about the Congo troubles in the newspaper, 'Whoever thought they could run anything', she said. As the flight went on they got quite friendly and she knowledgeably pointed out every farmhouse far below. Later the *Sunday Express* reported that John had been cut out of the will. John denied this to reporters, but in fact he and his immediate family had been excluded from the will which had been signed in 1956, five years earlier. Perhaps he knew that, because of the bad relationship between him and John's parents, the cantankerous old man had not intended to include him and so, in a way, had not cut him out. In fact the only family money he ever received was an annual allowance of £250 from the day he won the Sword of Honour in 1945 and the income from £10,000 settled by Charles Rudd on his grandchildren. Indeed there was no love lost between Ursula and Percy. She wrote to say, 'I see Percy Rudd is no more. Isn't it marvellous?' The outcome was that John, the scion of one of South Africa's most prominent diamond-trading families, received no significant inheritance.

In June, John wrote a piece in his diary which he thought he might use as a speech from the dock. He did not use it, but it is reproduced here as an example of his thoughts.

'I flouted the law of this wretched land. That is about all there is to it. Why? Because in all I saw of those obeying the law there was no love, but selfishness, no giving, but hogging, no spirit, just blind pathetic, wretched feeble resignation - resignation to wrong. The smugness of the whites verses the vitality of the blacks. I wanted to join the latter. I got more from and with them. I really did like them more, for what they were – real people, not layer upon layer of social and economic units, going through the motions of existence at whatever level applied. Africans were one vast pot, boiling and bubbling. Whites were little packets, dehydrated soup, waiting to be given life – but powdery, tepid, outrageously dull – in ghetto-like apartness from each other, the police, the threatening attitudes – the cloud getting bigger on the horizon.

What would happen if that was my defence? I flouted this law, feeling it evil, sympathising with the oppressed – not a gesture, nothing furtive, but the bulk of the State makes it impossible to achieve much more than a gesture. Where friendship exists it seems no law on God's earth can legislate on such matters. The effrontery of a State that says 'Thou shall NOT love thy neighbour', totally unchristian and these dishonourable people call themselves Christian.'

When the time for the appeal came round John was cautiously optimistic as he had heard that Mr Justice Clausen was to hear it. He was an adherent of

Moral Rearmament and John had come across him before. But Clausen turned the case down and it was taken by Judge Oscar Galgut, who was to prove unsympathetic. The prosecution counsel, Sugman, was sneering and aggressive. The fact that the panties were found under the pillow proved pivotal and John soon realised the case was lost.

John tried to persuade his mother to write a letter of support to Dottie, but to no avail. Ursula wrote later that it would be impossible for her to greet him on release from jail if, 'you go on with your friendship with that girl'

There was one legal option left open: a petition to the Lord Chief Justice. But the two of them decided to serve their sentences and so get the whole thing over. John spent the last few days saying goodbye to friends. On September 22nd he was back in *Mingary* on his own, and from the table on which Dottie had fallen he wrote her a love letter. It went, 'I've never loved anyone so much as you ever in my whole life. I think of you almost the whole time now. And you are fantastic to think about.'

Dottie wrote back, saying, 'Darling I am going to jail with you, dearest love, so that afterwards we can do anything we like – but let me tell you something, there will be no other girl that loves you just like me'.

He went shopping for prison, buying toothpaste and brushes, Lifebuoy soap, pants, vest, writing pads and biros. The assistant ironically said that if the things were not all right he could bring them back and exchange them. A member of the legal team had found out about the prison regulations. On arrival inmates could only take the clothes they were wearing and nothing else. These would be exchanged for prison clothes. There were to be no privileges for four months. This meant no letters or visits except legal ones on legal business. Luckily these were not strictly enforced. The maximum remission was one third.

There was a last supper at Gale House with Dottie, some of John's friends, Stanley Uys and the Laubschers. Tessa's mother, Louisa, an amazing woman with a large heart, was a terrific support to John at this time. Considering that an affair between the races must have been very strange to a woman of her generation, she was stalwart. Dottie, with glasses on the end of her nose, did an impression of Gush. She went, 'And you know, number two – you are a groovy girl – but you are not that young – you should know better than to get mixed up with Europeans. Just because you are young and a first offender and were dominated by the glitter of the stage, do you know what I am going to do for you? I'm sending you to prison for six months.' After this bravura performance she collapsed and was taken up to bed. The next morning John wrote to his mother and, to keep morale up, Robin would pretend to be a Guardsman and thump John each time he walked past. At eleven in the morning the two of them, fortified with brandy, set off with Laurie Penny. John was dressed in a grey well-cut suit and Brigade of Guards tie. At times they were recognised at traffic lights and Africans waved cheerfully. As they approached the Magistrates Court John put his hand over to Dottie and she kissed it. There was a battery of pressmen at the door and John issued a statement saying,

'Dottie and I are the victims of a despicable law which does not exist in any other country and which has nothing to do with the generally-accepted meaning of the word 'immorality'. It is a law which can cause a fantastic amount of anguish; probably more than any other law it bedevils relationships between Whites and non-Whites. Yet about one thing I am absolutely clear; no Government, and no law can ever succeed in destroying friendship across the colour line; for there are some things in life, thank God, that lie too deep for any lawmakers to obstruct for long'.

Once inside, John and Dottie had to part as the areas were segregated but they were reunited at the check-in desk. Dottie, slightly tipsy, was on good form and cracking jokes. Also John spoke to Stanley Uys, then reporting for the Johannesburg *Sunday Times,* saying, 'When I come out of jail I would like to carry on working with Africans in friendship and with a sense of common social purpose, especially in theatre, music and the arts. In this I am definitely not alone. Perhaps after this experience I will have an even clearer idea of what is at stake here.' He went on to say that some of his friends in Britain and the US had encouraged him to flee the country but he had rejected this saying, 'This is the country in which I was born and this is the country of my future. I pleaded not guilty to the crime of which I was charged because I maintain I did not break the letter of the law. I do not deny I have probably broken the spirit of the law in that I am guilty of forming a friendship with Dottie Tiyo. This government has made a law under which the least gesture of affection between a White and a non-White person can be stigmatised as "indecent". It is appalling that society condones this stigma.'

On arrival at the court their fingerprints were taken and then they went down to the cells. Gordon Winter, the controversial journalist who was once a spy for BOSS, the South African Secret Service, but later changed sides, writing for the *Sunday Express* reported that John called to him. 'Cheerio, see you soon'. John was apprehensive that at any moment Dottie would kiss him. As she walked to the cells she passed a cleaner with a broom and she gave him a pat and said, 'You know – this is what John will be doing.' At the final parting of the ways in the basement the two just shook hands. John was marched off to the European end and looked over his shoulder to see Dottie in her blue Italian jersey and grey black shorts led off to her end. She shouted, 'John, John' from 40 yards away and he wondered if he should blow her a kiss, then he made a sharp turn and she was gone. John was placed in a cell with the door left open which he shared with a timid fellow who was there for debt. Then about 10 prisoners were assembled and marched out into the back of a lorry with a mesh cover. One man had only one leg and they all scrambled to help him as if on a London bus. The prisoners chatted away in Afrikaans and John looked out for the truck that would take Dottie away. As they drove out

The Fort Prison, Johannesburg

he thought of other Saturday mornings when he would just be finishing at the De Beers office and returning to a pleasant weekend at Bryanston. It was a bumpy ride and the one-legged man fell off his seat and had to be scooped up. At the Fort Prison there was a long line of warders. Only recently had the establishment recovered from an outbreak of typhoid which broke out in the black section. John later discovered they had assembled to see this celebrity inmate arrive. From the reception desk they were directed to the whites' changing room. Only two of the prisoners were down for 'hard labour': John and a big fat-faced lorry driver called Joubert. The others were on remand and could keep their clothes. John had to change into a prison outfit of a pair of ill-fitting rubber clogs and grubby khaki shirt and trousers, which he managed to exchange for a better set later on. Then he was told to go and find a cell. It was strange he was not allocated one and he found one which he shared with Joubert and a sailor. Food appeared which was pork floating in cream of pumpkin. All this time he was thinking of how Dottie was getting on. For the rest of the day he was locked in.

Next day there started a routine of scrubbing floors or being locked up and, as it was Sunday, a service was held by the Salvation Army led by an evangelist with a concertina where both John and Joubert sang lustily. On Monday they were unlocked at 6am and John was given *The Sunday Times* and *The Star* to read, and he featured in the leading article in both. John, Joubert and a tattooed youth were sent off to the wood yard to chop wood in the sun with blunt axes. He managed to cut his eyebrow with a splinter and was sent off to the hospital to be stitched up. Later that day one of the prisoners told John of the tricks of his trade. He would take bank managers on fishing trips on the Natal coast and rob their banks the following week. John speculated about possible newspaper headlines, 'Rudd speaks, then Rudd sweeps'. That night he was put on kitchen duty and spent it making risottos. As time went on John got to know the Fort's governor, known as the Colonel. He gave John a bit of advice, telling him that Bantu were no good and that he should leave them well alone. There was an excitement when some inmates escaped. They dug a hole in the cell wall and then put blankets over the wire. John observed with amusement the warder on duty turn ashen white when he saw the hole. John heard news of Dottie from another prisoner. She had been promoted to prison monitor and was looking after the cats and canaries in the kitchen. He was also promoted to monitor and took to learning Afrikaans and Zulu. One of the jobs he was given by the Colonel was to go through *Who's Who in South Africa* and pick out the likely donors to the Police Orphans' Fund. He mused that in a year or so he might have been in it himself. He wrote to his mother to say, first, 'I'm OK', and then to report that the first few days were hell and humiliating but that his spirit had never wavered. He called the Afrikaners bullies and vowed to wage war on their leaders when he got out. He got on well with some of the prisoners but not the warders, whom he resented calling 'Sir'. He hoped she had received all the press cuttings that he had asked his brother Robin to send, which chronicled their surrender to the authorities when they went down 'guns ablaze'. In the letter he noted he had already done 10 days so, like the proverbial prisoner, he was ticking them off one by one. Turning to the positive side, he comments that incarceration gives him the clear insight into the iniquities of Afrikanerdom which would help him to wage war on it when he gets out. He ends by saying that David Schneider, his lawyer, has been wonderful and that all correspondence should go to him. David Veitch, John's best man at his wedding, who had been a stalwart throughout the saga, also wrote to Ursula reporting that John was fit and, as only he could do, making a go out of a difficult situation. David smuggled food in from an Italian restaurant and other friends would drop off provisions, honking their car horns outside the prison gates to let the inmates know it was ready. Jackie Kennedy, remembering John from his Guards Officer days, sent food parcels from the White House, which must have surprised the governor.

Ursula returned to her new home, *Les Augerez*, St. Peter, in Jersey and wrote to her son every day. They are charming homespun letters, which merit publishing in their own right, where island and family gossip are mixed with uninhibited criticism of the regime that had locked up her son. Every time a Nationalist politician is mentioned his name is preceded by the word 'loathsome' or 'swine'. When her furniture arrived for her new home from the Cape she wistfully unpacked John's portrait [see over] which had been painted when he was an Officer Cadet at Sandhurst with Eton College in the background and carefully hung it above her desk. In Jersey she and her second husband Wally Machel had a good social life often mixing with South Africans and Rhodesians, but she did not advertise her Rudd connection and so avoided controversies.

John's Sandhurst portrait

John was placed in a small single cell where he could just read from a 15 watt bulb. His fellow prisoners, although not in the same section, included the ANC member, Walter Sisulu, who was to be jailed seven times in the space of 10 years. Walter had a white father and, ironically for a man fighting against racial injustice, suffered from prejudice at the hands of some of his fellow ANC members.

A buzz went round the Fort when news got round that a captured terrorist was to join them. He was Benjamin Sisele, a Zulu from Fordsburg, who was charged with possession of explosives. About the same time, after some emergency, police rounded up about 170 Africans. Although the jail was segregated the white inmates could see these newcomers arrive.

Christmas was coming round and this filled John with mixed feelings. He read in the papers that champagne was being sent to him from London for the festivities but he was told he could not have it until his release. Both John and Dottie were given remission for good behaviour and after four months they were due to be set free. Dottie was let out at 5 am wearing a royal blue, short-sleeved jersey, a tweed skirt and open sandals and was met by friends and reporters from the *Post* newspaper. 'I would have liked to wear the pink-with-mauve dress, pink hat and white shoes which John bought me, but I was not allowed to' she told them. She had applied for a passport while inside and her plans were to go to England. She had gained 19 lbs in jail, while John had lost weight.

A few hours later, the governor asked John if he would like to leave from a side door of the Fort as there were about 30 press men at the front. John gave him some of his champagne and replied that he preferred the front so as to get the furore out of the way. But the governor himself wanted to avoid publicity and he invited Laurie Penny, who was waiting with a car, in for tea and then the two of them left by the East gate. The press reported that John looked well

POST

5c Registered at the G.P.O. as a newspaper FEBRUARY 4, 1962

Snakedancer and White friend freed — and POST was there when they met again...

...DOTTY TIYO, RUDD REVEAL PLANS

I'm FREE, I'm singing

● *Dotty was so happy to be out of jail yesterday morning that she sang. The song? "I'm free, I'm living." And Dotty, above, has her first cup of coffee yesterday, in POST's offices.*

By Can Themba and Harry Mashabela

'HI, DOTTY! HOW ARE YOU?" With these words John Rudd greeted Dotty Tiyo yesterday at a secret rendezvous in Fordsburg —hours after they had both come out of jail.

Snake dancer Dotty and White businessman John had just finished their jail sentence for breaking the Immorality Act at John's posh Bryanston home last year. They were jailed for six months but got time off for good conduct.

AFTER GREETING EACH OTHER, JOHN AND DOTTY WENT OFF FOR A PRIVATE TALK.

Later, John planned a grand celebration party at which Dotty would be present. Then he intends to go to Kimberley, where he was born.

Parents

And Dotty? She applied for a passport in jail and plans to go to England.

Early yesterday morning Dotty and John were released from jail in Johannesburg. John was met by relations and Dotty by POST's reporters.

Dotty's first worry on coming out of jail: "I want to say hello to John. We've arranged to meet."

After that, Dotty plans to visit her parents in Port Elizabeth.

The R100-a-day girl wore a royal blue, short-sleeved jersey, a tweeed skirt and open sandals as she walked out of jail. Later, at a house in Hillbrow, friends had a smart outfit waiting for her. Then followed a new hair-do.

Private reunion after 4 months

Townships

"I would have liked to wear the pink-with-mauve dress, pink hat and white shoes which John bought me. But I was not allowed to," she said.

Dotty, of "Tremor" fame, who earned R400 while featuring in the filming, vowed she would not live in the townships. "I've never lived there before," she said.

Dotty told me she was a member of the Union of Southern Africa Artists and that she would continue her career as a stage girl.

All in all, Dotty told me, she earned herself R2,000 in showbiz and modelling.

She has gained 19 lb. in jail. She now weighs 129 lb. When she went to jail Dotty was slender and only 110 lb.

Dancing

Dotty is keen to go back on stage but would rather try her luck in England. She said she practised Indian dancing while in jail.

John, on the other hand, looked pale and drawn when he came out of the Fort and has lost a lot of weight.

Before he went to jail John told POST: "Dotty and I are determined to fight for human dignity."

He attacked the Immorality Act as degrading and said he had a clear conscience. Earlier, he visited Dotty's parents.

YESTERDAY HE TOLD POST: "MORALLY AND SPIRITUALLY I AM STRONGER. I HAVE NO REGRETS."

● Mandela goes on a trjp — Page 2
● Monty's picture burnt — Page 3
● Indian, White bride speak — Page 5
● Unknown beats S.A. champ — Page 16

The front page of the Johannesburg Post reporting John and Dottie's release and was again wearing his Brigade of Guards tie and novelty cuff links. Three reporters had sprung out of a tree. One said pleasantly, "Good morning, Mr Rudd". John was heartened to be addressed as 'Mr' on the first occasion for some time. He gave a statement saying that the Immorality Act was coming into even more disrepute and that only by contact would black and white acquire the character, culture and inspiration for a better future for all. Next stop was Gale House where Louisa Laubscher, Tessa, her two sisters, and a number of friends were waiting to greet him. Later on John held a 'coming out' party at which the governor of the Fort was a guest. As is common with those recently let out, John had a terrible feeling of anti-climax, but he was not to allow these low spirits to hold him back for long.

As anticipated, on John's release De Beers relocated him to London and he was given the job of running the Industrial Diamond division. Dottie at first returned to her father's house in Port Elizabeth and resumed her stage career. The publicity helped her and, under Wally Herbert's management, she went to South West Africa. She wrote to John saying, 'Oh John, do you mean to tell me you don't think of me. If you don't you must be cruel. Anyhow I am missing you a lot'. Later, she was in Dar es Salaam where Wally appeared to abandon his performers and she wrote to John for help. Things improved when she moved to Kenya and she married a Mr Gallant and was expecting a baby. A Mr Brounliger from Germany offered her film work and she planned to go there after the birth. When in Cape Town she had seen Tatu who took her to the Varsity Ball, but, being black, she was refused entry. They went off to a theatrical shop and bought a European mask and wig and then they were allowed in. Tatu, when her husband was attached to the *Argus* news agency, met her in Nairobi in 1964. She was last heard of living in Swaziland but John's attempts to contact her there failed. Many years later he remarked to a journalist, 'My greatest regret is that we had no child – what a boy that baby would have been'. One might add, if it had been a girl, then, what a girl!

Behind John were the marriage to Tessa, the traumatic and sensational trial, and prison. He threw all his energies into this new life. Perhaps the world of industrial diamonds was not as glamorous as that of diamond mining and dealing, but it was new. The market for industrial diamonds was important for De Beers, for to prosper they needed to expand, and the key area was the United States. But there was a problem: the American antitrust laws were hostile to De Beers, who effectively had a monopoly of diamonds.

A friend at this time in London was Randolph Vigne. They had known each other back in South Africa when John had had to work hard to keep Randolph out of jail. He gave the impression of being a harmless academic Liberal and had been one of the founders of South Africa's only non-racial political party, the Liberal Party, and, with a few others, founded the African Resistance Movement which believed that armed struggle was necessary for the removal of the apartheid regime. Right-wingers burnt his house down and he was lucky to only receive a Banning Order. Eventually he had to flee the country, ending up, via Canada, in London. In 2010 he was awarded the *Order of Lithuli* in silver by President Zuma. While rebuilding his life in London, John helped him financially and he became godfather to Randolph's daughter, Lucy. John was a hopeless godfather, inattentive and the donor of inappropriate presents, in one instance giving a cigarette lighter to a teenager. He was a much better godfather to his nephew Henry, Robin's second son. With his son Johnny in tow, he would arrive at his school, Eton, in his large Mercedes and they would all enjoy a good lunch by the Thames. When Henry broke his back playing the Eton Field Game, a crude form of football, he would visit him in hospital. At outings he would stuff bank notes into Henry's top pocket and, when he went to work with De Beers as a diamond sorter, he lent him his flat in Mount Street, Mayfair.

often took him to the UN in New York. Jaime was divorced, with a Swiss former wife and three children. The romance was intense, he was introduced to Anna's parents and friends and they anticipated a wedding. Anna described him as the most gorgeous and glamorous man in the world; even her mother could not keep her eyes off him. But fate struck. Jaime's former wife arrived in Washington with a child in tow; there was a good dinner with wine. One thing led to another and nine months later there was one more little Spaniard to add to the list. Jaime came from an old and respected Catholic family and held an important diplomatic post. He decided to return to his family. Anna was broken-hearted. She gave up her job and New York flat and headed for London. With her was a fellow Swede who had also been a guide, Birgitta Bjerke, who is now a farmer in Wyoming; she set up home in a flat in Cadogan Square. This was the time to arrive. The Swinging Sixties were in full flight.

Anna and John had met briefly before when Anna was living with her father in South Africa and she attended boarding school there. When the two met again in London the chemistry worked. Indeed it worked quickly for there was a six week courtship and then a wedding at Caxton Hall. Anna remembers the wedding dress: a white Chanel suit of thick fabric bought in Paris with the help of a friend who was fashion editor of Harper's. Her mother, Kristina, who lived in Paris, was with them but was horrified by the match. She had always imagined a wedding in Sweden in the Church next to their summer home. The reception was at the Guards Club and the honeymoon a trip around the world, marred by Anna contracting hepatitis from a dirty needle following an inoculation.

Back in London Anna found a flat in Hyde Park Gardens where they entertained widely; guests included many De Beers executives and the Oppenheimers. At one dinner party Christine Keeler was a guest and she enlivened the evening by taking outrageous liberties under the table with her neighbour, a German prince. Then the owners put the flat on the market. Anna encouraged John to buy but he deferred as De Beers were also interested. This was out of character for John as he was not a De Beers 'yes man'. Indeed there was an occasion when he was editing *INDIAQUA* and he was told by higher authority to remove an advertisement for Jack Lunzer's Industrial Diamond Corporation because they were having a row with De Beers. John, being loyal to his old friend Jack, printed a black page and a cryptic message

John and Anna's wedding

where the advertisement should have been. To Anna's annoyance the company got the property and they had to move.

De Beers had yet to overcome the antitrust hurdle in the United States. Harry Oppenheimer and Ted Brown were leading for their team. Their argument that their near-monopoly of diamonds was beneficial for the whole industry was plausible, but then the ruby, sapphire or emerald industries were not hindered by free markets. Anna recalls mentioning in front of some De

Beers people that she had a Green Card which enabled not only her, but her husband, to work in the US. Very soon the newlyweds found themselves in a luxury flat in a fine brownstone building off New York's Fifth Avenue, with a generous expense account. 'New York was a good time' recalled Anna. They had a lovely home with lively entertaining. Anna could catch up with her New York friends and contacts who were also useful to John's career. The downside was that John did not really like the job. The company he worked for was insignificant and was in fact just a US front for De Beers. He had liked his association with the Oppenheimers, De Beers and the international status that went with it, but it was unlawful for either of these two to do business in the US. For kudos he relied on his father's Olympic fame and his grandfather's dealings with Cecil Rhodes. It was about this time Anna noticed a touch of Jekyll and Hyde in John's character. Something would trigger him off and he would lash out verbally. She put it down to pressure at work.

John was away a lot but this did not worry Anna; she was homebuilding and had many friends and interests. One evening they were holding a dinner party where Harry Winston, the leading American jeweller, was a guest. A call came through from one of Harry's aides to say Israel had been attacked and the Six Day War had started. Pandemonium broke out, with one guest sending out instructions for $50 million to be sent to Israel. John had a good reputation in the world of diamonds and Harry Winston offered him a job. He considered it but De Beers was his family and he could not leave them.

The attempt to resolve the antitrust problem in the US had hit a brick wall and John and Anna moved back to England where John took over running the industrial diamond division for Western Europe. They found a charming house in the Essex countryside near Thaxted where Michael and Eve Ward Thomas, old friends of John's, were neighbours. Eve was an author writing under the name Evelyn Anthony. She has fond memories of John. He was again a particularly neglectful godfather to her little daughter Kitty, giving more unsuitable presents such as an electric toothbrush. Eve recalls his contrariness. When they went to see the film *Tora! Tora! Tora!* no doubt in reflection of his love for Japan, he cheered on the Japanese as they bombed Pearl Harbour.

John and Anna wanted to start a family and they were becoming frustrated that nothing had happened, so they consulted a Harley Street specialist. It transpired that, following childhood mumps, John's sperm count was low. Although John was wary of this, artificial insemination was tried and it worked. In spite of being eight weeks pregnant Anna accompanied John on an exhausting business trip covering Japan, India and Russia. On a blazing hot day in Moscow they were stranded on the wrong side of Red Square by an important funeral. Suddenly it looked as though the baby was going to arrive. John approached a policeman who stopped everything, the army, the march and the hearse. They rushed to hospital, John maintaining the drama by smashing a loo seat and using a section to remonstrate with the grim-looking staff. In fact the baby did not arrive and Anna was able to give birth in London, which was what she wanted. Bevil John Charles Rudd arrived on the 1st August, 1968, after a difficult birth with forceps in the private Welbeck Street nursing home.

John continued to spend long periods away on business. Anna made her mark in Essex with her spectacular good looks and extravagant tastes, and her bright light attracted an Iranian, Mahmoud Reazi. The Reazi family were one of the richest in Iran and Mahmoud ran their mining interests. On meeting Anna he bombarded her with flowers, caviar and scent. It was a challenge for Anna to explain to John when he returned from his business trips why the house was brim full of luxuries. Unconcerned that Anna was married, in a moment of camel trading rare in the Essex countryside, Mahmoud offered John £1,000,000 for Anna. He wished to have a long-legged daughter with her, whose name was to be Lily. Anna was not consulted and, some years later, on recounting the story, she remarked that, as things turned out, John must have kicked himself for not accepting the offer.

John's career never allowed him and his family to settle anywhere for long and in 1969 he was relocated to Tokyo to take charge of the industrial diamond operations for Asia, the Pacific and South America. They kept their English house but Tokyo was now their main base. Aiko, a young Japanese nanny, was employed, and she christened her charge John John, a name that stuck for many years. John loved Japan but Anna hated it. They found a nice apartment and a Swedish interior decorator helped furnish it. But Anna never took to the Japanese. Entertaining was a trial. Japanese guests seldom knew what to say, much was lost in translation and they would either all speak together, or, as they liked to act in consensus, select a spokesman, then have a conference before anyone spoke. On a trip to London, Aiko, looking at the crowds in Oxford Street, asked where all the people where. She was used to the incredible density of Tokyo, another factor that annoyed Anna. They had every creature comfort, chauffeur, maid, secretaries, but John was spending much time in Hong Kong and after a year they relocated there. Anna's father was a resident in the colony with his new wife and the expat community there were much more to Anna's liking. They found a flat near Sheko, an old fishing village where there was space and fine sea views. John was still away a lot, and Anna met Jack Keen, a British officer in the *Seventh Gurkha Rifles*, at a dinner party held by her father. Jack was half Hungarian and very glamorous and they started an affair. Jack cleared the decks. He dropped his London girlfriend and his wife sued for divorce, citing Anna. She found him very physical while John was the opposite and she left her husband to live in Singapore where Jack was stationed. But they were on unsure foundations. When John came to visit his son and plead for the return of his wife all hell would break out and Jack, a Gurkha officer where there are 26 VCs in the brigade, feared for his life. Anna recalled this time as very intense and exciting but she was living on eggshells and after six months John persuaded her to return to the quiet of England with him. Jack followed but there were too many complications and she ended the affair.

Johnny's complicated birth had left him disabled and he needed special schooling: Anna found him a place at Boveridge House in Dorset. Meanwhile John launched a magazine, *Indiaqua*, a contraction of Industrial Diamond Quarterly. It was an immediate success and very well regarded. He combined interesting news about the industry, social gossip about the characters of the trade, articles on historic diamonds by Ian Balfour, Harry Oppenheimer's cousin, and spicy pictures of young ladies whose connection with the subject in hand was not always clear. John edited the magazine with great panache, and in it he found his true metier. It continued until he retired when, because it was so much his creation and would not be the same without him, it closed.

John and Anna were basically leading separate lives. He was seeing much of a young Australian girl, Trish Fullerton, and Anna had met a charming middle-aged Venetian aristocrat, Marchese Marino de Lagarda, nicknamed the 'Venetian Moor' by John, where love had blossomed. The romance between Trish and John was promising. They met at a dinner party given by a De Beers executive, Geoffrey Gellie, in Chelsea. John was 47 and Trish 29. The chemistry was working and they arranged for their travel plans to overlap. Nairobi was followed by Johannesburg, where Trish was introduced to contrasting evenings in the shebeens of Soweto and dinner at the Oppenheimers. Then they travelled to Zululand to meet Chief Buthelezi. John acted as a bridge between the Chief and Oliver Tambo of the ANC. Buthelezi could not support the ANC's call for armed struggle and economic sanctions. The two had parted company over this policy and were not speaking. John's list of contacts was amazing. They met Premier Vorster in Pretoria, then he showed her the old Rudd family home in Kimberley, and they witnessed the conditions of the blacks in the mines and the segregation on the Cape Town beaches. Trips were also made to the Victoria Falls, Rhodes's grave in the Matopos Hills and Bulawayo. John pointed out, because of his intrepid forebear, Charles Rudd, that the country should be called 'Ruddesia'. On a tour of India they were met by the Maharaja of Jaipur on a motorbike, and in Kathmandu John got down on bended knee, proposed, and was accepted. But there were delays with the divorce coming through and the strain persuaded Trish after three years to end the engagement. Once or twice after that they met up and, in spite of many fond memories, she knows she took the right decision. In time everyone disengaged themselves and John's divorce from Anna finally came through. The Marchesa sued the Marchese, citing Anna, and in 1978 she married him.

New arrangements had to be made for Johnny as he had to leave his Dorset school at 16. Anna favoured a move to the country but Marino preferred London, the focal point of his social life. The solution to this dilemma came when her father moved to Cape Town for health reasons. They found an establishment, Camp Hill in Hermanus, which was suitable and John, with the help of a local Swede, Lennart Parkfelt, found a fine Old Dutch farmhouse, *La Provence*, set in a 20 acre vineyard in Franschhoek, which could be his South African base. In 1981 John bought it. The farm had been granted in 1694 to Huguenot Pierre Joubert, who came from a wine area in Provence; an earthquake in 1969 had damaged the buildings and the current owner did not have the capital for repairs. Freddie Steytler, his son, a graduate in viniculture from Stellenbosch University, was retained as manager. New vines, Cabernet Sauvignon, Semillon Blanc, Sauvignon and Weisser Riesling, were planted and Freddie concentrated on the farming, adding olive and plum trees as well as vegetables and pigs. John concentrated on the marketing and was a founder member, with Achim von Arnim, of *Vignerons de Franschhoek,* the trade association for the area. Achim, born in South Africa, was the grandson of a German general. He and John had a lot in common and became firm friends. John would entertain here with great panache. When a visiting delegation of Russian diamond traders came, he hoisted the hammer and sickle on his flagpole and played the Russian national anthem full blast from speakers in the garden. There was a memorable occasion when a Japanese delegation came. John welcomed them in a speech which all assumed to be in excellent Japanese. Harry Oppenheimer turned to the interpreter to ask what had been said. He replied that he did not have a clue as it was certainly not Japanese. The performance was a bluff.

John and Johnny by the Sea

There were many visitors from the UK and abroad including Anthony Montague Browne and his second wife Shelagh. Anthony had been Winston Churchill's private secretary and later was found to be the natural father of the present Archbishop of Canterbury.

The property was a bedrock for Johnny when he was not away at school. He had a marvellous nanny, Pinkie, who became one of the family. When

La Provence: The house

The farm

Harvesting

Johnny visited her later in the Franschhoek township the whole neighbourhood came out and they had a party. John could be impatient with almost anyone but his patience with Johnny was infinite. In many ways Johnny defined John. His love for him was unconditional. Freddie and his family were particularly supportive of him and, like the characters in a play, John, Anna and Mario would come and go with a surprising degree of harmony. The relationship between Anna and John and the other men in her life, Maria de Lagarda and later Nick Ciolli, was extraordinary. It was an arrangement that worked. John never resented the others, Anna was often his hostess at important functions, and at times they were all together at Christmas.

But *La Provence* and all its activities was a drain on John's finances and in 1991 he sold it to Count Augusta, an Italian industrialist who manufactured helicopters. Shirley Parkfelt, Lennart's wife, gave a farewell dinner for John when he left. She recalled that she was very fond of him but found him an enigma and never understood him. His butterfly mind, when he would flit from subject to subject, she found bewildering.

CHAPTER FIVE

INCURABLE ROMANTIC

Towards the end of the eighties John was approaching 60, and retirement from De Beers was on the horizon, but he still had the verve and looks of a man 20 years younger. He then became romantically entangled again; a romance that was to set a pattern for a string of romances which all had one thing in common: they were all disastrous. Things would go like this: he would meet a girl, usually half his age or less, and invariably attractive. He would become infatuated, shower her with gifts and money, and think it was love. It is

Julie on the cover of Indiaqua

Julie also appeared on another cover in this photo with John

unlikely that his passions were ever reciprocated but the ladies in question often strung along with the arrangement for their own benefit. The outstanding example of this phenomenon was his marriage to Julie Rall. Few of his friends knew much of this marriage and he never mentions it in any of his autobiographical notes, but they were married on 21st June 1988 in Paarl in the Western Cape. He was 61 and she 30 and, as can be seen from the photographs, she was devastatingly attractive. Julie had been John's number two on *Indiaqua,* billed as Special Assistant and Researcher-Reporter and, to take advantage of her cover-girl looks, John twice put her on the cover of the magazine.

According to the notes left by John the marriage was a sham. She wanted a British passport and the UK residence that went with it and perhaps later meet an eligible Englishman and marry. Also John was to help with the problems of her brother, Christopher, who had become entangled with the law. John wanted an ornament to satisfy his vanity. She was his trophy wife and perhaps he harboured the wish that one day she would become a more normal wife. Showing both his charm and romantic turn of mind, he wrote to Harry Oppenheimer as follows:

My Dear Harry *25th June 1988*

I hope you and Bridget are very well. You were both in tremendous form in London recently.

I am in good form since I find I have become not only engaged but married this week. I hope you appreciate such a robust reaction to early retirement plan from Debid.

The luckless girl is Julie, formally Rall, who came to Brenthurst with the last Japanese industrial Safari party you were kind enough to entertain so fantastically, (See INDIAQUA 49). Hank will be surprised, pleasantly, that she wasn't after all a Safari fiancée only!

There is quite an age disparity but, 'Youth lasts much longer than young people think'; 'As we grow older we grow both more foolish and wiser at the same time', or 'The tragedy of age is not that one is old, but that one is young'. – I'll spare you more …. But we get on and life is fun.

I hope it isn't imposing too much on you to ask you if you could persuade De Beers to allocate a rather special rough from De Beers Premier or CDM for me to purchase. May I be forgiven for going straight to you?

A Sumitomo synthetic gem diamond provided by a fellow Safarist was her original engagement stone which I feel less appropriate than a natural would be!

Sorry to do this to you, Harry

Yours Ever

John

(Note: Debid stands for *De Beers Industrial Diamonds*)

Having written this letter and filed a copy, John never sent it, and we do not know if Julie got her special diamond. John also wrote the letter set out below to the immigration authorities. As things turned out it could not be more ironic.

Dear Sir

I write to advise that my wife, formerly Julie Susan Rall, whom I married on 21st June 1988, and I remain happily married. I further affirm that I have every wish of remaining so married into the future.

I trust this testimonial statement is sufficient for your official purposes and that the HM Government may provide my wife with the necessary permission to reside permanently in the United Kingdom.

Yours faithfully

B.J.Rudd

The couple moved to London and very soon the wheels were coming off the relationship. John would recount in numerous outpourings to his diary and in letters to his bride how she exploited him, how; in spite of his love for her, she did not love him and how she fooled around with other men. Julie got a job with the Estate Agents *Anscombe & Ringland* in West Kensington, and the list of her lovers was impressive; James Gilbey, a onetime beau of Princess Diana, Peter Diamond, a property developer, Johnny Pollington, the heir to the Earl of Mexborough, and Hugo Charlton. Hugo was an Old Etonian barrister in his thirties. He came from on old military family, originally from Northumberland, but his father, a retired Colonel who won the American DSC in the war, lived in Essex. He did a lot of work for the Green Party, rising to be their Chairman, but fell from grace when he nominated himself for a peerage. Recently he has been representing *Occupy London* following their sit-in in the City of London. At least John had a good relationship with Julie's parents, Harold and Jill. He treated Jill as a confidante and wrote outlining his woes and humiliations. One letter describes how Julie insisted on a gift of a diamond bracelet. He takes her out to dinner, but it is a *ménage a trois,* as a boyfriend comes too. On some occasions John has to pretend to be an uncle! The arrangements in the flat are extraordinary. John is banned from the drawing room while Julie drinks and smokes there with her escorts. He is banished to his own room where he listens to opera on the tape recorder. Julie leaves insulting notes on De Beers notepaper around the flat, one signed *Julie Charlton*. At 3am he is woken by Hugo getting up and leaving his marital bed. It would be beyond the ability of any psychiatrist to work out why an otherwise normal and successful man would put himself in such a humiliating situation. At this time John was skilfully editing *Indiaqua* and also arranging the refurbishment and public opening of the Rudd bungalow back in Kimberley.

At last John realised that the only sensible action was to end it all. He had a great discussion with Julie and followed it up with a remarkably generous letter. He suggests she marries one of her boyfriends and starts a family. The flat where she lives, 40 Wetherby Mansions, will have to be sold, from which she will get £10,000. He states that he has loved her dearly since they first met at Goldsmith's Hall in October 1987 and has been proud and happy to have married her, if only legally. But all good things come to an end, he goes on, each of them has served their purpose. She has gained British citizenship and residence rights. He has had his vanity satisfied. He plans to go on his way, enjoy his life and work, the vineyard at *La Provence* and the project to win diamonds from the sea bed. He looks back on the last 21 months as a remarkable experience, ending, 'With much love and best wishes for your future. You are still the most fascinating, beautiful creature, and I shall miss you .....'

They divorced in November 1989 and Julie did go on to marry an English gentleman, David Gerard Leigh, nephew of William Gerard Leigh, who for many years was chairman of the Guards Polo Club. They had a family of two children.

On the sale of *La Provence* John purchased the more manageable *Karbonaatjeskraal* at Bergplaas in the remote Karoo desert. Here he found full expression for his restless spirit. It was conveniently set just off the main N1 road which headed north, not far from the sleepy railway town of Touws River. Here, with the help of 'chatelaine' Elsabie Andrews, he entertained paying guests, farmed ostriches and kept ponies and peacocks. A kloof led from the farm to a great rock pool where, surrounded by dassies, a small mammal related to the elephant, hiding in the rocks, troops of baboons would come down to drink. There was a swimming pool overlooked by trees full of weaver bird nests, where swimmers would find that numerous frogs had got into the water first. There was a ravine arising by the farmhouse which stretched back into the mountains to a small lake. General Smuts and his commandos escaped up it during the Boer War. John converted the barns into guest rooms and an old water tower was restored as a 'think tank' where guests would enjoy a champagne breakfast in the sky. Andrea Weiss, a journalist on

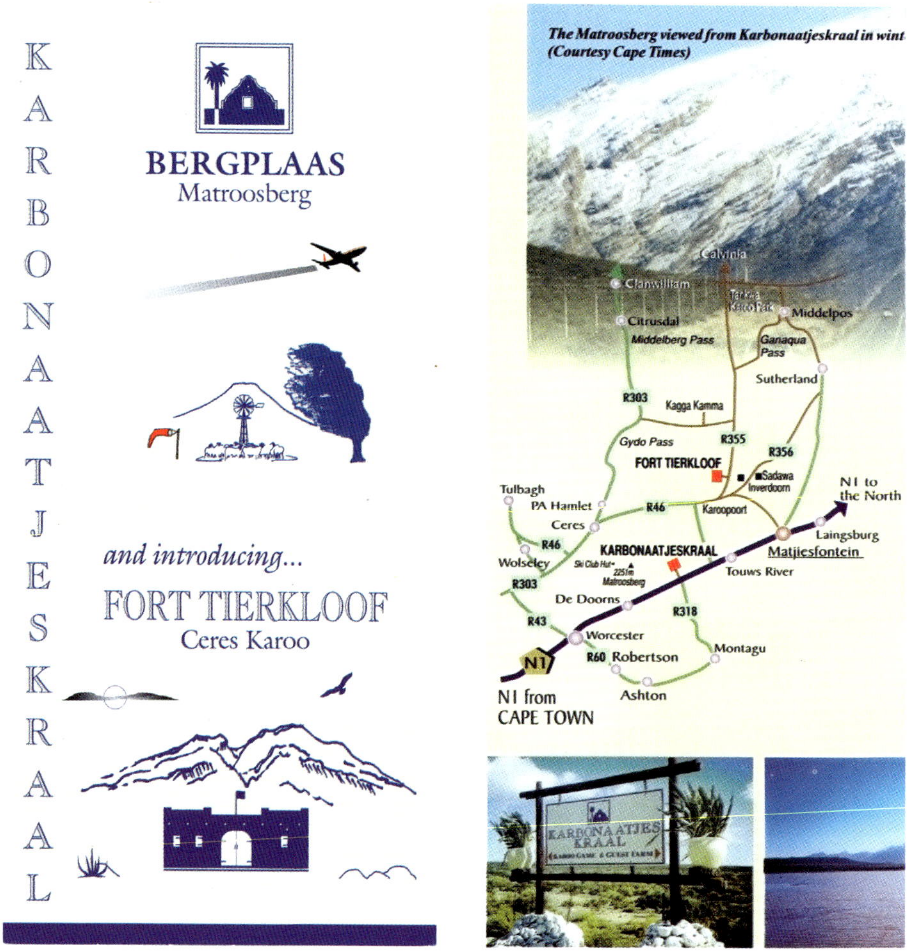

The Brochure for Karbonaatjeskraal

the *Cape Argus,* has many happy memories of staying there with her young family. The numerous barns, pools, gazebos and towers and weaver bird nests were a fascination for her children, but the greatest amazement was John himself. Periodically, he would disappear. Once, on New Year's Eve, he drove himself to nearby Worcester thinking he had had a heart attack, but it was a false alarm. The relationship between him and Elsabie was a mystery and often at night he was not to be found anywhere.

One of Andrea's abiding memories was of John taking the children up the mountain to a gazebo in his Toyota van, with her daughter Mary standing in the back belting out 'We Are The Champions'. Not content with this exotic

The farm in winter

creation, John trumped it with *Fort Tierkloof*. This was once a 200-year old shepherd's hut on the slopes of the Swartruggers Mountains, which he transformed into a French Foreign Legion fort. There were no neighbours except a native shepherd, his family and sheep, who all looked as though they could do with a square meal. There was no electricity, but guests would be treated to Black Velvet as they watched the desert sunset. The name came from the time when leopards caught the game that came to drink the water in the pools besides the Bushmen's caves. John waxed lyrical in his description of the fort in the brochure he produced. He wrote: *'A vast landscape unfolds below stretching afar to the distant Ruggerveld Berge. Tierkloof may be terra incognita today but a century ago it was the trodden path of Hottentots, Bushmen, the Khoi and the San and Dutch and British explorers seeking the interior. Already Karoopoort was the major staging port in the 1870s for horse-drawn mail, mule trains and ox wagons making their way to the Griqualand West diamond fields. On this scene now float flamingos on the lake at Inverdoorn where giraffes, zebra and wildebeest roam free.'*

On leaving De Beers John joined up with Dr John Gurney, a professor of geochemistry at Cape Town University, to launch Benguela Concessions, a company whose object was to mine undersea diamonds. They attracted some substantial investors and obtained a Stock Exchange quotation, but there was a snag; the technology did not yet exist for such mining. Unlike his great grandfather's ventures, the enterprise did not make a new Rudd fortune.

In April 2002 John organised a reunion for all the Rudd clan at the Kimberley bungalow to celebrate his 75th birthday. Interestingly, the invitations were headed by his name and Anna's, as indeed they were for an important function at *La Provence* a few years earlier. In many ways, in spite of all the vicissitudes, Anna was to remain the woman in his life. The reunion also commemorated the centenary of Rhodes's death, the end of the Boer War and the departure of Charles Rudd for Scotland. All four of his nephews came from various parts of the world as well as Nicky Oppenheimer and his wife Strilly. Guests visited the De Beers Shooting Box and enjoyed champagne at the Rudd bungalow. There was a special slide show illustrating Charles's life, an evening tour of Kimberley including the Big Hole, and a lunch at the Kimberley Club. Chief Buthulezi sent a congratulatory letter. The Oppenheimers had to return to Johannesburg and, breaking the rules, they did a fly past by the Kimberley Club in their helicopter, with John's sister-in-law Alison and nephew Henry as passengers.

As John grew older he was involved in a series of entanglements where, depending on your viewpoint, he was either an incurable romantic or a silly old buffer. Perhaps he was like Linda in Nancy Mitford's *The Pursuit of Love,* who always felt that the most recent love was the love of her life. There was Katarina, whom he met when he was 78 and she was 22. She worked as a waitress and he wrote '*I fell under your spell the moment you emerged from 45 Vyggies (a restaurant) in your pink flimsy blouse and black skirt, and you looked incredibly beautiful, though disdainful of your taxi driver*'. The roundabout would spin. John would support the young lady financially and would write letters overflowing with devotion and flowery compliments, but interspersed with complaints that he was ignored. Other waitresses were found at a cabaret bar, *Evita's*, run by Pieter-Dirk Uys in Darling, a

John in characteristic pose at his 75th Birthday Party in Kimberley

small town about an hour and a half north of Cape Town. One girl, Rhonda, required money to help with her family; John contributed and then wrote to say he felt unappreciated. The manageress had to take things in hand. In reply to an email requesting a booking she confirmed the reservation but pointed out he was to have no contact with Rhonda, Denise or any of the waitresses. John replied apologising for his behaviour and professing that he was just a 'fan'. He took Robert Loder on a visit to *Evita's,* pointed out a young coloured girl behind the bar and confessed that he was in love with her. Robert thought he had gone quite mad and was not surprised to hear he had been warned off by the management. Included in his constellation was 24 year old Eraldine, a waitress at the *Eland's Bay Hotel*.

John had to go into the Kingsbury hospital in Cape Town for an operation on a vascular leg. It was a success but they had to remove his left big toe. It was also thought he might have had a stroke, but nothing was to stop him. The last Dulcinea of this aging Don Quixote was Marie Persent, a 34-year-old mother of two boys, 15 and 11, whose husband Evelyn was treating her badly. John helped her with a divorce, paying the legal bills. He wrote to her saying 'I'm one who loves you so much and is alarmed for your safety'. In a

Although Fort Tierkloof was remote and had no neighbours, John managed to gather this assembly to celebrate his birthday

letter to a friend he reported that he had found love and described her as an absolutely striking coloured girl, witty, charming and brainy, with a German grandfather. We do not know what Marie thought of her 82-year-old boyfriend with a dicky heart and a missing big toe.

In February 2009 John was still helping Rhonda from the *Evita* cabaret bar with bills from her child's nursery school, but there was some other man in her life who wanted him out of the way. He wrote to say that if he was not wanted he would break off contact. He wrote to Marie describing how his health was deteriorating: he could stand up but needed a wheelchair to move around. He sold *Karbonaatjeskraal* and there was much trouble completing the contract as the purchaser had difficulty finding the money. He kept up the Fort, and was living there and in a little apartment in Worcester. While at the Fort he regularly met up with an old friend, Bob Holden, who lived in a most romantic but solitary spot on an artificial lake, *Lakenvlie*, above Ceres, where he was responsible for keeping an eye on the dam and the water levels. John wished to write his memoirs, a task encouraged by many of his friends. He was well set up to do it. He had kept copious notes, diaries, letters and photographs chronicling his eventful life. But time was against him and, anyway, he had never had the persistence to finish any of his writing ambitions. On August 30th 2009, his friends John and Annette Seekings visited him at his Worcester residence. John had written a biography of Charles Rudd and Annette, a trained nurse, could see from the condition of his legs that he was suffering from serious heart disease. He had told Anna that he did not want to live on in a decrepit state. He had been an active and vibrant man all his life and was not happy with his condition. The next day he died.

There was an impressive memorial service held in the old white church in Franschhoek with tributes or readings from five different Rudds, including a photographic montage put together by his great-niece, Pippa. Tessa dramatically arrived late, just as Miriam Makeba's singing of *Back to the Moon* from *King Kong* was being played. She commented that it was just like walking back into 1960s Johannesburg. The two wives then sat next door to each other, chatting and exchanging notes. Two girlfriends were also there, glaring at each other. An excellent tribute was given by Achim von Arnim. A trumpeter played *The Triumphal March* from *Aida* and the celebration finished with *The Battle Hymn of the Republic*, when the organist was so carried away that people felt the slates would fall off the roof. In the congregation were many sharp-suited De Beers men and also Chief Buthelezi. John Gurney, John's partner in the venture to find diamonds at the bottom of the sea, gave a tribute. John's character, he said, was multi-faceted, indeed the facets numbered more than you would find on a brilliant cut. One could list some of these: he was loyal, funny, unpredictable, rebellious, incorrigible, charming and exasperating. Donations were to go to Camphill where Johnny is looked after when he is not with his parents.

Six months later in Kimberley, on John's birthday, Anna arranged a series of events and an interment in the local cemetery next to John's father's grave. Friends and relations met in the Kimberley Club for lunch, there was a tour of the now silent mines where Charles Rudd first met Cecil Rhodes, and a service in the Rudd bungalow, now restored to its former magnificence, where Father Roger Hickey, a friend of John's and a Roman Catholic priest, held a service. They all assembled by the graveside. It was appropriate that John's ashes were interred next to his father in the same red earth where his ancestor had found those early diamonds, diamonds that had been such an important part of John's life.

Jackie Kennedy's letter of 2.1.1949 to John Rudd

Jackie Kennedy was 19. Knowing her interest in Cecil Rhodes, John had sent her an original of one of his letters. This is her reply:

Dear Bevil

I was terribly surprised and thrilled to get your letter with its precious content. I don't see how you remembered this long, and I think it was very nice and brave of you to send anything so valuable thousands of miles across the sea to a creature who might never send it back!

I can't tell you how exciting it was to hold the letter and think that Cecil Rhodes had touched the same paper almost a hundred years ago. It made it so much more real and now I worship him more than ever. My family descended on it *en masse* and my father has seen twice as much of it as I have and keeps muttering, 'Jacqueline, this is much too precious a thing to be entrusted to anyone as careless as you'. So knowing that, I'm sure you will breathe an enormous sigh of relief to have it safely in your grasp again. I copied it very carefully and plan to flaunt it at my history teacher when I get back to that dreary college, and pray that it will make him a little more impressed with me than he has been in the past.

As we left England this summer we tore round Europe so fast it was unbelievable, but it was all so perfect that I can't wait to get back, either this summer or next winter. In either case I'll surely come to England and hope I'll see you.

Miss Shearman[1] was not half so chipper in the end as when you saw her. Two of us bought dogs in Paris. Mine is a heavenly little poodle that has developed a thousand incurable diseases the French vets never told me about, and poor Miss Shearman is allergic to animals. She sneezed all the way home, and was so glad to get rid of us in New York that she zoomed down the gang plank and disappeared over the horizon before we could ever say goodbye to her.

It is really quite dull to be home again and all I do is reminisce about the time the two Italians chased Helen and I down the bell tower in Florence, of how beautiful Paris was, and of lovely cold London and the powdered eggs!

Thank you again Bevil so much for sending me the letter. You don't know how much I appreciated it and if your article ever materializes I should love to see that too. Give my best to Rupert[2] and if there is anything I can do over here, do let me hear from you.

I am terrified that this will never reach you – that the plane will crash, the boat sink or something, but I shall keep my fingers crossed.

As ever

Jacqueline

PS. I lost the envelope your letter came in so I have no idea if you are a Lieutenant, Captain, Major or what! – and hope the Coldstream Guards won't think this addressed in too unmilitary way.

[1] Miss Shearman was Jackie's Latin teacher at her school in Washington and her chaperone for the trip.

[2] Rupert is almost certainly the Hon Rupert Strutt, a son of Lord Belper and a fellow officer of John's in the Coldstream Guards.

Index